I0152034

# BEYOND
# WORDS

*A Radically Simple Solution*
*To Unify Communities,*
*Strengthen Businesses,*
*and Connect Cultures*
*Through Language*

## JAMES B. ARCHER JR

FOUNDER OF THE **SHARELINGO** PROJECT

© 2017 James Archer

All rights reserved. No part of this publication may be reproduced, distributed or transmitted in any form or by any means, including photocopying, recording or other electronical or mechanical methods, without the prior written permission of the publisher, except in the case of brief quotations embodied in reviews and certain other non-commercial uses permitted by copyright law.

www.Archer.com/beyondwords

For orders, please email
OrderBeyondWords@archer.com

# Help start a million conversations.

All profits from the sale of this book will be used to aid organizations that support cultural inclusion and foster respect for diverse races, genders, religions, countries of origin, and sexual orientation.

For example:

The Robert A Miller Educational Resource Center

Jeffco Action Center

One Colorado

Latina Safe House

Open Media Foundation

Casa de Paz

*For Blaine and Samantha*

For Gloria and Samantha

# TABLE OF CONTENTS

FOREWORD     1

INTRODUCTION     5

1.0 We're the SAME     9

2.0 Who Is This Book for?     19

3.0 What Is Culture?     29

4.0 Stereotypes     43
    *4.1 It's time to stop wasting talent*     *58*
    *4.2 How do you feel about U.S. workers sending money to Mexico or China?*     *62*

5.0 Do Immigrants Even Want to Learn English?     65

6.0 Sector/Industry Examples     75
    *6.1 Hospitality*     *76*
    *6.2 Construction and Landscaping*     *82*
    *6.3 Healthcare*     *91*
    *6.4 Education*     *99*
    *6.5 Law Enforcement*     *105*
    *6.6 Faith-Based Communities*     *111*
    *6.7 Nonprofits*     *120*
    *6.8 Sales and Service*     *125*
    *6.9 Love and Family (and Dating)—Wait. What??*     *130*
    *6.10 Government*     *136*

7.0 How to Learn a Language     145

8.0 How Does ShareLingo Work?     157
    *8.1 The ShareLingo Model*     *157*

8.2 *The ShareLingo Method*                                161
8.3 *The ShareLingo  (or Other) Materials*                 170

**9.0 Conclusion**                                         179

**ACKNOWLEDGMENTS**                                        181

**ABOUT THE AUTHOR**                                       183

**II. How ShareLingo Started**                             189

**III. If I Didn't Speak Spanish, I Would Have Missed a Great Opportunity**                                          195

**IV. Should I Still Learn Spanish?**                      199

**V. Mara's Story**                                        202

# FOREWORD

When I step in front of my university classes this fall, I will take a moment to welcome the Spanish speakers in the class in their native language. I have not been able to do that before, but when this summer ends, I will have learned enough Spanish to confidently start that conversation, thanks to classes I am taking this summer at ShareLingo.

The ShareLingo program is taking me further, faster than the four years of high school Spanish and the occasional trip to Mexico. Once a week, I sit down with four other English speakers and five Spanish speakers. We pair up and help each other pronounce and understand phrases and sentences that are important in everyday conversation.

As an educator, I appreciate that ShareLingo is founded upon sound adult learning theory: appealing to learners' intrinsic motivation, making lessons that are relevant to learners' personal goals, breaking a complex process into bite-sized chunks, and providing opportunity for learners to teach each other.

In a recent class, Saraí listened carefully and corrected my pronunciation, and I did the same for her. The ShareLingo method has made it easy for us to give and receive picky feedback. We follow a set pattern of modeling our language, correcting our partner's speech, interpreting phrases, and converting English into Spanish (and vice versa). We often go off into tangents and marvel about the intricacies of each other's languages. This is so much more enjoyable than conjugating verbs or talking into a computer.

Saraí is a young immigrant professional working as a restaurant cook. I am an older college professor. We never would have crossed paths if not for this weekly ShareLingo class. But my life is richer for knowing her, and I hope I am helping her get ahead in our English-dominant work world. I hope that her current and future employers recognize the fresh perspective she brings to the workplace — a perspective that builds workforce cohesion and improves customer satisfaction; a perspective that becomes ever more critical as our country becomes more multi-lingual (albeit reluctantly).

At my university, Metropolitan State University of Denver, about one-fourth of the student body is Hispanic, and many of them speak English as a second language. I teach public relations and journalism — fields that require a lot of writing — and I am amazed at and admire the assignments turned in by these Spanish speakers. If only I could write Spanish half as well as they write in English.

Even so, they require a lot more coaching than my native English students. I believe I will be a better resource to them once I can meet them on their terms—literally. And I believe I and the other English speakers in our classes will improve our own storytelling once we gain more understanding of the Spanish language and the cultures that speak it.

Welcoming my Spanish-speaking students in their language is just my first goal. The goal after that is to teach/learn from Spanish speakers in the immigration detention center in Aurora, Colorado. Did you know that in 200 jails and private prisons around the country, immigration detainees are held in limbo for months or years? Some are legal permanent residents who have families in this country. Others are victims of human trafficking or are seeking asylum from torture or death in their home country.

In a country built upon due process and freedom from government oppression, 400,000 people are held without bail or a clear path to freedom. This has gone on under my nose since the '90s. I don't know what I can do about it, but the first step is to meet and understand the people my country has warehoused in these gulags, and to help them tell their stories.

I believe we can change the world one conversation at a time. I found a like-minded person when I met James Archer three years ago. At the time, I directed a communications and marketing program for a very large health organization, and James was beginning the ShareLingo Project. He had made his living as a computer engineer and was launching this language program with the ultimate goal of bringing people together through face-to-face communication. My organization was in the process of extending health insurance coverage to the uninsured, many of whom spoke Spanish. ShareLingo helped our sales team gain functional competence in the language, enabling them to reach prospects that our competitors could not.

So I see how ShareLingo will make me a better teacher, how it will help me do my part for social justice, and how it has helped an organization increase sales. I hope this book helps lay out a feasible path for you to break down the language barriers in your world.

In the end, this is all about individuals taking action to make a difference. I believe we all have the desire to make our world a better place, but that we often do not know how to take the first step. I believe you will find those first few steps in the pages of this book.

> *"Never doubt that a small group of thoughtful, committed citizens can change the world; indeed, it's the only thing that ever has."*
> *— Margaret Mead*

Steve Krizman
Assistant Professor of Journalism and Public Relations
Metropolitan State University of Denver
June 22, 2017

# INTRODUCTION

Odds are, a language barrier is holding you back. It's preventing your organization from achieving its potential, or it's standing between you and the people you want to help, or it's closing you off from meaningful conversation with someone important in your life.

Why DON'T you speak that other language? Did you take it in high school or college? Have you started an online course and not completed it? Have you found yourself in Mexico fumbling through your restaurant order, wondering where all that language study went?

You know the answer: you need to practice. I have found a way for you, an English speaker, to get practice with a Spanish speaker who needs to practice their English. And it's not as hard, scary, or time-consuming as you might think. I have found how this process can benefit not only individuals, but businesses, communities, neighborhoods, and our society.

I founded the ShareLingo Project some three years ago as I was learning Spanish myself, and have since brought hundreds of people together to teach each other their native tongue. I have helped schoolteachers reach a level of conversation that smooths their communication with parents. I have seen manufacturing and service industries eliminate language barriers to improve customer satisfaction and workplace safety. I have seen a father of the groom honor his new in-laws by giving his reception toast in Spanish.

This book tells the stories of dozens of businesses, nonprofits, governments, and individuals that have made significant, measurable impact by participating in the ShareLingo program. (Many names have been changed.) We focus on Spanish now, because it is the second-most-spoken language in the U.S., and because it is my own personal interest. But I look forward to the day when ShareLingo expands to other languages. Maybe you can help me get that started.

*(Pew Research Center http://bit.ly/BWStats1)*

After you read this book, you will have the ability to overcome that language barrier that has been holding you or your organization back. You will have a plan of attack and be able to proceed with confidence, knowing that others in your situation have succeeded by using this method.

Like those pioneers, you will increase profits, broaden your market reach, delight your customers, improve the lives of others, and learn to speak Spanish yourself! And like those pioneers, you will gain the satisfaction of knowing you have made the world around you a richer, more harmonious place.

Read on and find out how it is that you have made this language barrier a bigger beast than it is. You don't need to be fluent before you can achieve your personal and business goals. What exactly IS fluent, anyway? (I'll explain that, too.) You really can learn the Spanish you need if you set appropriate goals and focus your practice. That's the secret of the ShareLingo method, and the growing ShareLingo family.

Thank you for being here.

# 1.0 We're the SAME

*"The mystery of human existence lies not in just staying alive, but in finding something to live for."*
*—Fyodor Dostoyevsky, The Brothers Karamazov*

## LINKING THE ENGLISH- AND SPANISH-SPEAKING COMMUNITIES.

**You speak Spanish?**
**I speak English.**
**We're different.**

I probably am a lot like you—or you're like me. I believe that we can all be friends regardless of race, religion, country of origin, gender, sexual orientation—whatever. I KNOW this is true, and I bet you do, too.

Where we may be different is, I found my passion—my mission, my calling—somewhat later in life.

But this is it. I'm here. I'm in the right place. I'm helping to connect communities and break down fear and misunderstandings. And this is what I am meant to do.

I want to show you how, so if you want to, you can do it too.

This book lays out what I've seen since starting The ShareLingo Project—a social enterprise that helps connect English and Spanish speakers to practice together. With it, you will be able to follow my roadmap and start to change your world.

## Why Spanish?

The United States has more Spanish speakers than Spain. Actually, the U.S. has the second highest Spanish-speaking population in the world, behind only Mexico.

Are you surprised? Many people are. And did you know that Spanish is the world's second most spoken native language, and English is the third? Only Mandarin Chinese has more native speakers.

In the United States, it's now cool to speak Spanish (actually, it's cool to speak any second language, but especially Spanish). It helps with your mission, your business, your travel, and even your love life. People on the street told Rosetta Stone (http://bit.ly/BWVideo1), "You can't get much hotter than an Argentinian!" One wondered how to say "pretty woman" in Spanish. All were surprised to learn:

- Only 9 percent of Americans speak a second language, whereas 65 percent of people outside the U.S. speak a second language

- Only 5.5 percent of world's population speaks English as a primary language

- 85 percent of executive recruiters say it is absolutely necessary that you speak a second language to succeed in today's international business market.

So, it makes sense to learn some Spanish.

**Are you ready?**

But this book will not teach you Spanish, or English, or any other language.

This book WILL show how you can learn Spanish AND about other cultures AND make new friends AND grow your business. By following the ShareLingo roadmap, you will find yourself sitting down face-to-face with someone who is as interested in learning English as you are in learning Spanish.

This book is focused on helping bring the English- and Spanish-speaking communities closer together by demonstrating how sharing language and culture, face-to-face, can help both sides. Participants not only learn each other's languages, but also about their cultures. They become friends.

In chapter 6, I give you many examples, for many different industries, for how this is possible.

In chapter 8, I break down ShareLingo's model, method, and materials so you can implement a ShareLingo-style program within your own organization.

And this will lead to less fear—less distrust—i.e., more peace. And if you are in business, it will also lead to increased profits. Yes, you can "DO GOOD" at the same time you are increasing profits.

## Why am I doing this?

Why would I share what has taken me so long and cost me so much to create?

There's tension in the world right now. In our country. In our cities. In businesses. In fact, 77 percent of Americans say the country is divided on important values (Gallup, http://bit.ly/BWStats2).

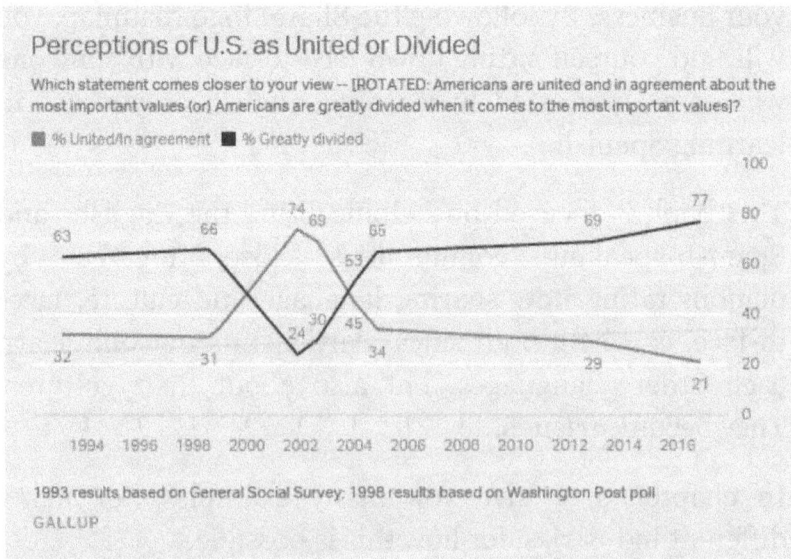

### Perceptions of U.S. as United or Divided

Which statement comes closer to your view -- [ROTATED: Americans are united and in agreement about the most important values (or) Americans are greatly divided when it comes to the most important values]?

■ % United/In agreement   ■ % Greatly divided

1993 results based on General Social Survey; 1998 results based on Washington Post poll

GALLUP

*See TED talk—Robb Willer—How to have better political conversations. (http://bit.ly/BWVideo4)*

Perhaps you see the tension within the school where your kids go, or in your workplace, or even your church. If people are afraid, there is tension. If kids are crying in schools—and they are—there is tension.

Nowhere is that tension, fear, misunderstanding greater than between the English- and Spanish-speaking communities.

> Maybe your school is holding pot-luck dinners to gather everyone together. If that is the case, that's great!! But my guess is, all the English speakers go to one side of the gym, and all the Spanish speakers go to the other.

How can we build empathy, or even hear the other side's viewpoint, if we don't even speak the same language? And I'm talking literally, not figuratively. Translators? Think about being in Paris, or Munich, and having to have a translator to talk to your doctor. It's not the same—not nearly the same—as being able to communicate with them directly.

Without conversation, how will we ever address the tensions in our country?

This book is not intended to take a position on any political topic. Not on race, religion, gay marriage, or immigration. It is quite emphatically the opposite. I want to bring people together **regardless** of their race or political views. I've SEEN conservatives and liberals getting along. I've seen Black, and White, and Brown, all laughing and helping each other. Gay, Lesbian, Muslim, Jew, Catholic—all that can drop away in the moments that we **talk with** and **teach** each other.

**The ShareLingo Project offers a solution.**
**It's working.**
**So I want to share it.**
**That is the purpose of this book.**

*The ShareLingo Project brings English and Spanish speakers together to share both language and culture. Participants normally meet for two hours, once or twice a week, for 10 sessions. ShareLingo provides a method and materials, so the people don't sit in the room and stare at each other. "OK. Talk!"*

*Depending on the location or organization where we are helping, we may also provide a bilingual facilitator. The members get to know and trust each other. They become friends. And this leads to real conversations. A real exchange of points of view. A real sharing of perspectives. This in turn leads to higher morale, less staff turnover, better guest/client satisfaction, increased safety, and increased efficiency.*

## Let's connect cultures

Throughout this book, I will mention Spanish over and over. That is because Spanish is the second-most spoken language in the world, and because the ShareLingo team is hyper-focused on that core tension in our own community here in Denver, Colorado.

**But I want to make it clear that the principles and benefits that I speak about in this book apply to ANY two languages or cultures.**

In some U.S. communities, the tension may be between English-speakers and those who speak Russian, Vietnamese, or Arabic. In Brazil, it may be between Portuguese and Chinese. In Canada, perhaps it's between speakers of English and French.

And let's not forget the tension between English speakers and English speakers. Or Spanish speakers and Spanish speakers. *Wait, what?*

Can we help build friendships between English-speaking Whites, African Americans, and Hispanics? Yup. How about friendships between Mexicans, Colombians, and Cubans, living here in the United States? YES! Please read on to find out how this program helps in THAT respect.

## Political correctness alert!

I've been known to refer to English speakers as "Gringos" (not politically correct), "Americanos" (but, isn't Colombia part of America? Colombians think so), and "Anglos" (not accurate).

I've also been known to use "Hispanic" and "Latino" interchangeably, although I do know the difference. I talk to Spanish speakers in both Americas daily. But I think political correctness has gone way too far. In English, we don't have adequate words for "English Speaker" or "Spanish Speaker," so I just don't sweat it.

The problem is, these words mean different things to different people. While Gringo is not offensive to me, someone from Nicaragua would never call me a Gringo—because it's such an offensive term to THEM.

If you come across a word I've used in this book and it offends you, please save yourself the umbrage and just mentally substitute your own term for whichever term that is. No offense is ever intended.

And you can call me a Gringo if you want to. I don't mind.

Again, the ShareLingo model works across all languages and cultures—across all (adult) ages and economic levels. It builds RESPECT and UNDERSTANDING between the participants. *Understanding* has every bit as much to do with culture as vocabulary.

*"I've never seen a program that can connect our community like this one does. ALL races are welcome and engaged."*
*—Jocelyn Miller, Executive Director*
*Robert A. Miller Educational Resource Center, Denver, Colorado*

*"It's like a club in which everyone grows together."*
*—Abram Palmer, Facebook review*

## Are you in?

This book is based on what I have learned while creating and implementing ShareLingo's programs for individuals, schools, and businesses.

If your business or organization needs to implement any sort of cultural inclusion program, there is enough information in this book for you to start a program yourself—in your school, your business, your church, your neighborhood, or your non-profit.

But if you need any assistance, I hope you will call us at ShareLingo. We can help you.

By implementing a ShareLingo-style program in your organization, you will be helping to start the conversations that we so desperately need right now. This will help your community. But it will also help YOUR ORGANIZATION in real, measurable ways. This kind of program is not a cost! It's an investment that will yield huge rewards.

You've probably been thinking about this problem for a long time—don't wait any longer. Now, more than ever, it is critical that you help break down these barriers. We CAN all be friends. I've seen it.

Please read on!

WELCOME TO THE SHARELINGO FAMILY.


**You're learning English?**
**I'm learning Spanish.**
**We're the SAME.**

# 2.0 Who Is This Book for?

*"We hate some persons because we
do not know them; and will not know
them because we hate them."*
*—Charles Caleb Colton*

Do you—or does your organization—regularly see a disconnect between English and Spanish speakers? Maybe they literally cannot talk to each other due to language differences. Or maybe "not understanding each other" is more of a *cultural* disconnect.

Either way, you can help change that. You can help eliminate the fear and misunderstanding between these communities.

My goal for *Beyond Words: A Radically Simple Solution to Unify Communities, Strengthen Businesses, and Connect Cultures Through Language* is to give you plenty of information for you to start your own ShareLingo-type groups within your organization. The little stories that I tell—along with the breakdown of model, method, and materials—will help you do it yourself.

So, who should read this book?

Well, of course, I hope that EVERYONE will read it. Every author hopes that.

But I'm not trying to reach EVERYONE.

I'm just trying to reach YOU. One person.

You are someone who wants to, or has to, address the English/Spanish language and cultural disconnect.

More than likely, you are reading this book because you, or your organization, deals with this disconnect on a daily basis. Perhaps you're a nurse trying to help your patients. Maybe you are a pastor reaching out to a divided community. Or maybe you're a teacher or school principal trying to reduce the achievement gap and help your kids get the most out of learning and life. Maybe you're an HR professional tasked to "Fix this problem!"

Who are you?

Do you see yourself anywhere on this list? *(This is a long list—so just scan down and see what you identify most closely with.)*

## Education

Are you a principal, trying to reduce the achievement gap in your school?

A teacher who just wants to communicate with immigrant parents?

On a school board, trying to cope with the fear in your district right now?

## Healthcare

Are you a doctor/nurse who wants to communicate directly with your patients?

Are you involved with a non-profit that is trying to help immigrants understand the health and social services available to them?

A first responder who needs to communicate fast? *(Where's the translator?)*

## Social or Human Services—Nonprofits

Do you help the disadvantaged?

Are you trying to help the Black, Brown, White, or Asian communities understand their rights or access public programs?

Do you represent the LGBTQ community and want to reach Spanish speakers in that community?

Do you believe it's important for everyone to vote— and to understand what they're voting for?

Do you care about the environment?

Do you need to enlist the huge Spanish-speaking population in your cause?

## Faith Community

Are you a pastor who wants to connect multiple communities in your church?

Are you organizing a mission trip where learning some Spanish would make you VASTLY more effective?

## Construction/Landscaping

Are you looking for better efficiency?

Do you need to improve safety on the job site?

Are you bringing in H2B workers every spring?

Are you looking to find or retain more local workers?

## Hospitality

Is there a disconnect between your front desk and service staff?

Are guests upset they can't talk to housekeepers?

Are housekeepers upset they can't talk to guests?

## Food Prep and Services—Restaurants

Do you hear a lot of "Kitchen Spanish" every day?

Are more and more of your customers Spanish speakers—or do you WISH they were?

## Manufacturing

Management and Shop Floor

Do you have English/Spanish speakers who are just at odds with each other, or even antagonistic?

Do you have production problems because of inefficiencies, errors, or misunderstandings?

## Professionals

Are you a lawyer, accountant, or other professional who is starting to see more and more Spanish-speaking clients?

Is your one bilingual receptionist not up to tasks like marketing, social media, and sales?

## Salespeople

Do you wish you could capture part of the $1.5 trillion Hispanic market that is waiting for you?

## Government

If you work in federal, state, or local government, whether you are elected or appointed, you owe it to yourself and your community to read this book.

## Military

Are you about to retire or leave the service (thank you, by the way, for your service) and you want to retrain before joining the civilian job market? (Speak Spanish!)

Are you stationed overseas? Do you want to engage with the community?

## Self-Employed

Do you have your own business? Are you ignoring 25 percent or more of your potential customers? Or are you encountering customers every day who do not speak English?

## Unemployed

Do you want to re-career?

> If you're retraining to get a better job—don't forget language.

## LOVE—Romance—Travel

> I know this is not really a "sector," but the truth is, if you are attracted to foreign people and places, this is a very strong motivator for learning about other languages and cultures.

## I know, it's a long list.

The disconnect between English and Spanish speakers affects almost every sector, and the need in our society is huge!

So again, let's narrow it down to just YOU.

You are not in ALL of these sectors. You are probably in just ONE, or at most a couple.

I have included lots of stories and examples in Chapter 6. I hope that one or more of them will resonate with you and help you improve whatever issues you are dealing with between English and Spanish speakers. Doing so will also help improve our communities and the lives of the immigrants you help to connect.

### *Is SPANISH not the problem you are facing?*

*I know that here in the United States, and throughout the world, there is a need for a ShareLingo-type program for many languages besides Spanish. Someday, ShareLingo will help with other languages also. We just don't have the bandwidth to do that yet. Maybe YOU do. If you have a huge need within your community or organization for a different language, I hope the examples and methods in this book can help you to start your own mission! Please contact me—I want to help in any way that I can.*

But today—it's about YOU. You're that person on the "front lines," so to speak. The one who wants to "end the war" and help bring our communities together.

And you want to make a difference.

### Who is this book NOT for?

I have chosen not to address the topic of undocumented immigration within this book. While I do have a very strong opinion on the subject, I think I could write a whole different book on that subject alone.

But I will go so far as saying I am very pro-immigration, and pro-immigrant.

This book may not be something everybody will choose to read. A lot of people may take one look and decide it's easier to send me hate mail than to understand the purpose of this book.

Go ahead—send me the hate mail. But I hope you're brave enough to also send your own contact information. By doing so, you are agreeing to receive a response, and you just might be starting a conversation with me.

When I outlined this section, I was thinking about White Supremacists, Black Activists, Muslim fundamentalists, Christian fundamentalists, and yes, even some of the Hispanic/Latino activists and organizers. (Organizing is a good thing, but being militant doesn't help the community.)

Some people, even some friends of mine, may be uncomfortable with the idea that I would invite members of those types of organizations to talk with me and to start a conversation. Some will say, "How can you even TALK to those people?!"

Well, everyone thinks they are right, and that the other side is evil.

Most agree that this all stems from fear, which itself stems from a lack of exposure to alternate views.

I recently ran across another great TED Talk idea that I think sums it up.

There are THREE sides to every argument. We can all play a role in helping defuse even the most bitter conflicts. In the article, veteran negotiator William Ury shares his hard-won insights.
*http://bit.ly/BWVideo3*

The only way we will reach common ground is by starting to talk to each other, right?

Well if there are language barriers adding to the problem, this book is for you.

It won't happen overnight, but we can start. So even if—maybe *especially* if—you are part of one of the groups above (the "Hate Groups"), and even if you don't want to read another word in this book, let's start talking to each other.

Reach out to me. I won't preach or judge. I'll listen to your point of view. But I'll probably also share mine. That's the deal.

Either way. Whether this book is FOR you, or NOT FOR you, I hope you will reach out to me, or someone, and start a conversation.

And if you want to help start LOTS of conversations, please read on.

# 3.0 What Is Culture?

*"Preservation of one's own culture does not require contempt or disrespect for other cultures."*
*—Cesar Chavez*

### Culture | Definition of Culture
### by Merriam-Webster

**Definition** of **culture** for English Language Learners: the beliefs, customs, arts, etc., of a particular society, group, place, or time. : a particular society that has its own beliefs, ways of life, art, etc. : a way of thinking, behaving, or working that exists in a place or organization (such as a business)
*http://bit.ly/BWResource1*

Certainly, people from different countries have different cultures. But as the definition above suggests, even a "place," such as a business, can have a different culture *(Management vs. Shop Floor)*.

And is it fair to say that there can be a different culture between police officer and civilian? Doctor, nurse, and patient? Teacher and parent?

Boston and Mississippi?

Culture means all kinds of things. Sharing our cultures is critical right now.

Think about YOUR culture. Actually, you probably have several "cultures."

MY cultures are these:

- I'm a fifty-(uhm, something)-year-old white man.

- My grandfather was Czechoslovakian, and my Grandmother was from Wales.They lived in Iowa. I have a Midwest accent and Midwest "values."

- But also, my father was career Air Force, so I grew up all over the world.

- Once grown, I lived in Canada for a bit and Australia for a longer time. I've also lived in Italy and, for a couple of months, in Colombia. And, of course, I've lived in the United States for most of my life.

- I'm an engineer—Talk about being different!

- I'm an entrepreneur.

- I'm super interested, and pretty active, in social causes.

- I speak Spanish (which I learned late in life) and I love MANY aspects of the Latino culture.

How does this relate? Let me give you an example. I grew up in a military lifestyle. So I understand that culture. I know what it's like to live on an Air Force Base—to shop at the commissary (the military grocery store), to play ping-pong with all the enlisted personnel, as well as eat in the Officer's Mess with the Generals. I get that culture, and I can talk to them, relate to them, and feel comfortable with them. I don't have any FEAR when I approach the front gates of a military base or post.

I'm also very comfortable going to Hispanic meetings and events, because I've had an opportunity to experience so many of them.

But I've never lived in Brazil. Never even been there, (though I desperately want to someday), so I have no experience of the culture to draw upon. And I don't speak Portuguese. Which means that if I went to Brazil on my own, I might have moments of fear. I might be caught "out of my element." Going with a friend, though—a friend who might have grown up in Brazil—could change everything. THEY have a window on that culture, and they can share it with me.

As you think about YOUR cultures, think about all the ways that your past, your education, your family, food, and music, influence your culture and how you think. Think of the parts of your life that have taught you your life's lessons. Think about how you can SHARE those cultural insights.

Now think about all the things you would love to learn from OTHER cultures. Try to be broad. This could be that you want to learn about people and places in Africa! But it can also mean you want to learn about the different "cultures" where you work.

**Please, don't be "color blind."**

This book will not encourage you to be "Color Blind." Just the opposite, in fact. I don't like that phrase. I want to be, and I want ShareLingo to be, "Color Aware." We acknowledge different people—not just color—but religion, sex, or sexuality. Our message is that it is not just OK to be different, but wonderful.

- Do I treat my Black, Hispanic, Asian, or Gay friends differently? No.

- Do I ignore that they are Black, Hispanic, Asian, or Gay? No.

Diversity. Inclusion. Acceptance. Whatever your keyword is, it's wonderful.

I'm an engineer, as I've said previously. But I appreciate artists so very much. I think that is because I am not an artist. I can't dance, or sing, or play an instrument, or draw even a stick figure. So I LOVE artists. Wouldn't the world be a terrible place if it were filled only with engineers? But, wouldn't it be a terrible place without us?

Diversity. Differences. We need those.

**The "Lingo."**

Every culture—whether from different countries, or different occupations—has its own "Lingo."

lin·go

ˈliNGgō/

*noun*

1. a foreign language or local dialect.

2. *"they were unable to speak a word of the local lingo"*

**Hot Pink**

The other day, we were working with a group from a large landscaping company (we'll talk about them more later in this book). We were talking about colors. This is very important in the landscaping business. Before digging, a surveyor sprays colors to mark lines: blue for fresh water, yellow for gas or steam, red for electricity, and so on.

One of the participants tried to translate "Hot Pink" literally as "Rosa Caliente." Everyone laughed because in Mexico, "caliente" can have the connotation of promiscuity. But the Spanish speakers were genuinely curious about if we really called that color, "Hot Pink." One of the Mexicans in the group called the color Rosa Mexicana—"Mexican pink." But that didn't work for the Colombians and Hondurans in the group.

Everyone was looking at the same color. But people had different names, according to their own lingo.

Another area where you REALLY see different "lingos" is in the military. Everyone speaks English. But the Navy has words and phrases they use. The Army has others. And the Air Force others still. Each branch has its own lingo that members of that group or "culture" understand.

**When we <u>share</u> our <u>lingo</u>, we open a window to our culture.**

### The Family Tree

We seem to be losing the family unit here in the United States. And even when our families stay together, we ship the kids off at age 18. Being an empty-nester seems to be something to be happy about.

That's not normal.

In most of the rest of the world, the family is critical long past the age of 18. There's a good reason for this.

In many countries, there is no government assistance. If you don't work, you don't eat, and you die—unless you have family to take care of you.

Do not confuse generosity with charity. I know many, many generous Latino people who do not donate to charities. That's not part of their culture. That's part of our culture.

Often, this extends to the community. If they know someone in trouble, they will be super generous. If you come to their house, they will share whatever food they have with you—even if it means everyone else has to eat less. "If there is food for 10, there is food for 15."

But they don't donate to "causes" so much. This does not make them bad people. It certainly does not make us better than them. It's just two different cultures and two different ways of helping the needy.

If you are "family," they will give you everything they have.

To illustrate the importance of family in Latino culture, as well as the way language, or "lingo," is a window to the culture, let me show you something.

| English | Spanish |
|---------|---------|
| Sister-in-law | Cuñada |
| Mother-in-law | Suegra |
| Son-in-law | Yerno |
| Daughter-in-law | Nuera |

| | |
|---|---|
| Step-father | Padrastro |
| Godfather | Padrino |
| Godmother | Madrina |
| No word for this | Compadre |

In the Latino culture, the family is so important that each position in the family tree has its own word.

And if you are one of the millions who believe, because of the old western movies, that "compadre" simply means "friend," it's actually much more than that.

If you agree to be the Godfather of my child—meaning that, if I die, you agree to take care of them as if they were your own—we become compadres. Co-parents.

I think that's beautiful.

I find it beautiful because it demonstrates a fascinating contrast to my "home" culture. The dominant U.S. culture is what's called "low context"—we value individualism, have many, looser relationships, and are very rules-oriented (note all the legalistic language in our familial relationship titles!). Latin cultures (and many Asian and Middle-Eastern cultures) are "high context," with emphasis on family and work-team connections; where they nurture fewer but more intense relationships, and where decision-making is more situational and intuitive. *(See description of Edward T. Hall's "Beyond Culture" here: http://bit.ly/BWResource2).*


## When I go to a Mexican Restaurant.

I love going to Mexican restaurants.

First, because I love the food. Denver has the best green chili in the world.

(No arguments, any of you!)

The second reason is I get GREAT service.


Person brings glass of water.

Probably doesn't acknowledge me.

I say, "Hola, ¿Cómo estás?" [Hi, how are you?]

*Lots of people can get this far. So they're not impressed.*

"Bien, bien," [Very well] they reply, just to be polite.

THEN I start a conversation:

"¿Cómo te llamas?" [What's your name]

Eduardo, Jose, Maria, etc

"Soy James. Mucho gusto." [I'm James. Nice to meet you.]

"Mucho gusto. ¿Donde aprendió español?" [Nice to meet you. Where did you learn Spanish?]

"Aqui, en la calle, mas o menos." [Here, on the street, more or less.]

"Oh, wow. Hablas muy bien el español." [Oh, wow. You speak Spanish very well.] *(What you may not catch here is they changed from formal Spanish to familiar. That's big. That's bonding.)*

"Gracias. ¿De dónde eres?" [Thanks. Where are you from?]

"De Chihuahua." [From Chihuahua (Mexico).]

"Ah, hay mucha gente in Denver de Chihuahua! ¿Por cuánto tiempo has estado en Denver? [Ah, there are a lot of people in Denver from Chihuahua. How long have you lived in Denver?]

"16 años." [16 years]

"Bienvenido/a!" *(Big SMILE)* [Welcome! *(Big SMILE)*]

"Gracias! Si necesitas algo, estoy a tu servicio." [Thanks! If you need anything, I'm at your service.]

At this point, I have them. I've established that I'm welcoming, and friendly, and I've made an effort to connect with them. It changes everything! We're instant friends. If I want more water, or salsa, or queso, or salsa verde, they're all over it.

The next time I go to that restaurant and get that mesero (waiter), they remember me.

Is this little story more about language, or culture?

The waiter/waitress probably speaks English. Or, at least enough so that I could have had that brief conversation with them in English. In their minds (and the minds of most Americans) there is a language barrier—but in many instances, that's not really the case.

The Cultural Barrier is far stronger.

The reason they don't engage in a conversation with me from the beginning in English isn't generally because they don't know enough English. It's because, fundamentally, they are scared of me. I'm from a different culture. And maybe they haven't always had the greatest experience with people from my culture.

By me embracing their language and trying to speak it, I am also expressing a familiarity with—an acceptance of— their culture.


**Look at me. I'm talking to you.**

Here in the United States, we value eye contact.

But what many Americans don't understand is that most other cultures are just the opposite.

When I was growing up and my Mom or Dad wanted my attention, they would say, "Look at me, I'm talking to you." They wanted me to focus on them.

When a child from Mexico, or Colombia, or China, or Italy is growing up, and especially when they are in trouble, their mother or father may say, "Don't look at me! I'm talking to you."

The child is to look at the floor, or their hands, or anywhere but eye-to-eye. If they were to look at their parents eye-to-eye, it would be taken as defiance.

*"Bring it on! Give me your best shot!"*

Now—what happens when the two cultural differences collide in the form of a job interview? An immigrant is interviewing with an American manager.

The manager is asking questions: "What's your name? Where have you worked?"

Where does the immigrant look? At the desk. At the floor. At their hands. Anywhere but directly, eye-to-eye, at the manager.

**THEY DO THIS TO SHOW RESPECT.**

What does the American manager think?

*This person won't even look me in the eye.*
*They must be dishonest. They must be lying.*

By painting someone else with our own cultural norms, we introduce our own bias into the mix. We may not even know this is happening.

Addressing a cultural difference like this requires education.

1. We can let the manager know that looking down is an immigrant's sign of respect.

2. We can let the job applicant know that eye contact, in our culture, is very important.

Even better, we can let the two of them explain it to each other. Then it really sinks in.

The ShareLingo model can help you connect people from different cultures so they can learn from each other.

YOU can learn more about someone else at the same time you are helping THEM understand more about US.

# 4.0 Stereotypes

*"I don't believe in stereotypes.
Most of the time, stereotypes are just that."*
*—Javier Bardem*

There are two big stereotypes in particular that I would like to dispel:

1.  "All the immigrants are poor, uneducated farm workers draining our system."

2.  "All the Americans hate us immigrants."

If you're reading this book, I'm sure you know that neither of these is even remotely accurate. They are misconceptions fueled by hatred, rhetoric, and ignorance. This isn't a new thing. Our history is filled with this type of talk. The Irish, Germans, Chinese, Italians, Japanese, Pakistanis, and others have all suffered the stereotyping.

But if we look past the rhetoric—past the polarizing, politicized sound bites—we will find something different.

I hope this chapter gives you a few facts and insights that can help you counter these stereotypes the next time you hear someone on either side bring them up.

**All the immigrants are poor, uneducated farm workers draining our system.**

Yes, many immigrants who come here start out poor. And many don't.

I attend lots of networking events around Denver. Naturally, lots of them are in Spanish-speaking communities.

Remember that many immigrants (meaning, not just Hispanics) came here and started out poor. If you look back to the Irish, or even the British who settled here, you will see countless stories of poverty and hardship.

But the immigrants today—the ones who do come here poor (and not all of them come here poor, as I will show below)—are they really a drain on our system? Are they all uneducated?

> First, undocumented immigrants do not qualify for welfare, food stamps, Medicaid, and most other public benefits. Most of these programs require proof of legal immigration status, and under the 1996 welfare law, <u>even LEGAL immigrants cannot receive these benefits until they have been in the United States for more than five years.</u>

Even non-citizen (legal) immigrant adults and children are about 25 percent less likely to be signed up for Medicaid than their poor native-born equivalents, and are 37 percent less likely to receive food stamps, according to a 2013 study by the Cato Institute. *(This infographic showing the path to legalization will boggle your mind: http://bit.ly/BWResource11.)*

Guess what—many who start out poor start their own businesses—from food services, to construction, to cleaning, to auto mechanics. There is an "American Dream" mentality within the immigrant community. They're creating jobs, paying taxes, and yes, learning English.

I sat down with Agnes Talamantez, a Mexican American who grew up in San Antonio Texas. Her parents didn't really want her to speak Spanish. There are many generations of immigrants who were not allowed to speak their native languages when growing up. We did the same thing with the Italians, Germans, and many others. But through education and lots of travel and working with other cultures, she managed to hang on to her roots and is 100% bilingual.

Over the past 30 years or more, Agnes has helped many thousands of immigrants start and grow their small businesses. In addition to working with individual clients, she teaches courses, holds workshops, and has a radio show (in Spanish) to help people learn about business-related topics.

I've known Agnes for several years and have been on her radio show, but for this book, the tables were turned. I got to sit down and interview Agnes for a couple of hours. She's a fascinating woman with a fascinating story and viewpoint on many things. She's lived with discrimination most of her life.

I could probably write a whole book just about Agnes and what she's experienced. But I don't have space here.

The golden nugget that I want to share with you from the interview is this:

Agnes has noticed that Americans don't really like risk. Yes, there ARE entrepreneurs, like myself. And you could argue that the vast majority WISH that they were entrepreneurs. But in reality, most Americans need stability and structure. They have a fear of jumping off the cliff. They need to know that a check is going to come in every month—and frankly, if that's not from a job, then it's normally going to be from unemployment or welfare.

As Agnes points out, immigrants have taken the biggest risk of their lives. Many have come here with only the clothes on their backs—or possibly one meager bag of belongings—to start over in a new country. *(Would you do that?)* They are ready to work. The risk of starting their own business is trivial by comparison. They just want to know HOW.

And this is what Agnes helps with. She teaches them about forming a company, banking, insurance, and paying taxes. I'm trying to encourage Agnes to write her own book about some of the many success stories she's seen.

For those who are not starting businesses, the desire and motivation to find employment is strong. This is a positive cultural bias that the talk shows and detractors paint exactly backwards. Immigrants are not a drain on our system.

I do not want this book to be about documented vs. undocumented immigration. But in doing research for this book, here's something I found interesting: According to CNN Money, if it were not for the undocumented workers who pay into the social security system but do not qualify to receive benefits from the system, social security would have had a shortfall (not been able to pay all the baby boomers) starting back in 2009. As all the baby boomers start collecting social security instead of contributing to it, we need as many young workers as possible to make up the shortfall.

Immigrants DO pay taxes. They have federal and state withholding, like any American. They buy groceries, gas, clothes, cars, and even houses. The U.S. Hispanic market is approaching $1.5 Trillion in value. The reason you see Tide, Ford, Coke, and McDonalds commercials in Spanish is that it is a POWERFUL and SUBSTANTIAL market.

How about the next question: are all these people uneducated? Are they all just picking crops? No. Not at all. Many educated professionals also come to this country. Some get to work in their chosen profession, but many do not. I see doctors, accountants, engineers, and systems analysts cleaning houses and hotels if that is what it takes to feed their families. They work at McDonalds. They work in construction. Here in Denver, if it snows, immigrants, to a large extent, are the ones who are out there at 4 a.m. shoveling our sidewalks and paths.

I'm at a client's place to do a class for their English and Spanish speakers. Thursday afternoon, Basic 1 class. It's been snowing for about an hour. None of the Latinos show up for class. "Where is everybody?" I ask. "It's snowing—they're getting ready. They'll be out all night shoveling."

And the big question: are the immigrants "taking American jobs"?

According to the CNN Money article mentioned above, as well as my own observations, immigrants tend to fill the jobs that Americans do not want.

The CNN article states, "Immigrants, regardless of status, fill the growing gap between expanding low-skilled jobs and the shrinking pool of native-born Americans who are willing to take such jobs. By facilitating the growth of such sectors as retail, agriculture, landscaping, restaurants, and hotels, low-skilled immigrants have enabled those sectors to expand, attract investment, and create middle-class

jobs in management, design and engineering, bookkeeping, marketing and other areas that employ U.S. citizens."

I saw this for myself just last Friday. In Chapter 6 below, I'll tell you about METCO, a $50-million-a-year landscaping company. They do everything in their power to hire locally. But on Friday, I helped them process nearly 300 H2B visa workers who were arriving from Mexico to work for the Summer. As I point out in that chapter, METCO wouldn't do that unless they had no other way to get the workers that they need. And on Friday, dozens of full-time METCO staff—managers and foreman and bookkeepers—were helping to process the new workers. Without these workers, most of these managers wouldn't have jobs.

Culturally, the immigrants I meet do not expect handouts from the government or the community. In their countries, the government doesn't give handouts. If you don't work and your family doesn't look after you, you starve. WE teach them about "entitlement." WE teach them that they should ASK for free products and services. They don't come here thinking that way.

I was talking to a fellow after a meeting at the Hispanic Chamber of Commerce where I was doing a presentation. He is a welder and owns a company that does everything from handrails on houses up to pipeline work out in the gas fields. His name is Jesus, and yes, he's an immigrant. He made this point to me:

"There are many homeless people here in Denver who stand on street corners and ask for money. I believe it's pretty common throughout the U.S. Here's the thing—if you drive all over the metro area and count all of the Mexicans who make up these people on the street corners asking for money, I bet you wouldn't fill up one hand."

I hadn't made that connection before—but I stopped to think. And as I drove to my office, I took a closer look at the people on the corners—of the 20 or so people I saw asking for help, not a single one was Hispanic.

And now, as I drive all over this town, I notice, and I almost never see Hispanics asking for help. I DO see them all over town, including on street corners. But not asking for handouts. They may be running a taco stand, or selling oranges and fruit, but they're never, in my recollection, asking for something for nothing.

Next question: are they all "uneducated?" Not at all.

In many sections of this book, I talk about professionals who have to take jobs outside their professions in order to survive.

It's hard for professionals like doctors to get accredited here in the U.S. It's possible by going back to school or jumping through lots of (sometimes expensive) hoops. The Spring Institute for Intercultural Learning *(http://bit.ly/BWResource4)* is one organization that is helping with the process.

Paula Schriefer is the Spring Institute's President and CEO. She and I have met many times over lunch or at various events. We share lots of goals and dreams relating to breaking down cultural barriers and helping the community. I guess technically, Spring Institute and ShareLingo might be considered competitors, but we are in an industry where we are all pulling for the same causes—so rather than resent each other, we offer each other encouragement and help.

Paula was kind enough to connect me with Ben Juston, also from the Spring Institute. Ben specifically works with immigrants who have medical training from their home country get certified in the U.S. The stories he told me about the process they have to go through were just depressing.

If you are a doctor from another country and you want to become a doctor here in the U.S., you basically have to start over. And the deck is stacked against you. First, you have to restudy for and pass new exams. Those exams can cost over $2,000, not including books and training.

Then, you have to go through residency again somewhere. But the hospitals that have residency programs don't really want you—because they have tons of applicants from universities they already work with. So you have to interview for any residency program that you can, which may mean flying, at the drop of a hat, to whichever city a hospital is interviewing. This is just for a CHANCE at gaining entrance. More thousands of dollars.

As you can imagine, many immigrants don't have the kind of money this process takes. But if they try to get a loan, it is a personal loan, not a student loan.

Despite those headwinds, the Spring Institute helped five foreign-trained doctors obtain residency matches in 2017. Overall, the institute's Colorado Welcome Back program has helped 700 foreign-trained doctors, nurses, and other health professionals navigate the U.S. credentialing systems.

From a recent Spring Institute newsletter (reprinted with permission):

Meet Jessica, one of our foreign doctors who applied and was matched this year. "Obviously, the language was probably the biggest challenge for me," she commented. "Luckily, I found the CWB (Colorado Welcome Back) program at Spring Institute, which has been a great help. Ever since I discovered CWB, they helped prepare me for my interviews and guided me through the process, which was extremely long and complicated. It was very competitive to get into programs in Colorado, but I met a lot of people from other countries through the CWB program. Some of my closest friends here in Denver are the ones I met through Spring Institute. I'm so thankful for them and know that we'll be friends for life!"

Even if immigrants don't come here with college degrees, the vast majority still value education. The immigrant community, and the Hispanic community in particular, are making up a larger and larger percentage of students in higher education.

> Our own Metropolitan State University here in Denver has seen its Hispanic student population grow from 12 percent in 2007 to 24 percent in 2017. The university has actively sought to serve the Hispanic community, reaching out to high schools, developing an inclusive campus environment, and becoming the first Colorado university to provide in-state tuition to undocumented students who came to the U.S. as children and have grown up as Americans in Colorado schools. It is on the verge of earning a federal designation as a Hispanic Serving Institution, which it will achieve when its Hispanic student population reaches 25 percent.

## The EB5 Visa

First: what is it?

Put simply, someone who wants to move here from another country can obtain a visa by investing $1 million (or in some distressed areas, $500,000) in a business venture. They have to create a minimum of 10 full-time jobs, and maintain them for at least two years. After that two years, the applicant can apply for permanent residency. Some investors choose to open businesses themselves. But many contribute via a Regional Center.

Here's a simplistic example of how this can work. Suppose a developer or investment manager wants to build a new hotel or senior housing development. They can seek traditional capital, or they can create an EB5-compliant business plan and seek overseas investors. Each overseas investor applying for the EB5 visa is "allocated" a percentage of the investment. The project, including all jobs created and maintained, are documented in order to demonstrate the investor's contribution to the project.

Does anyone actually do this?

Yes—LOTS!

For example, Dallas/Fort Worth has seen many of those immigrants moving into that area, buying big houses and big cars, and embracing the community.

Why would someone want to do this? I can't speak for the Chinese or Russian or other applicants, but I do know what's happening with many Hispanics.

Suppose you own a concrete factory in Mexico City, or Venezuela, or El Salvador. Maybe it's been in your family for years. It employs a lot of people, and it makes a good profit. Everything's great, right?

Except that your family has to have bodyguards every time they go anywhere. You're watched everywhere you go. You're scared. And mostly you are scared for your kids.

So you move your family to Dallas, or some other city in the U.S. You invest in a business there. You buy a house. Now your kids can walk to school, play in a park, have a dog. You can pop back to your country if you need to, but mostly you can run the business back home from the U.S. After two years, you can apply for permanent residency, then sell your share of the business you invested in, hopefully for a profit. After five more years, if you choose to, you can apply to be a citizen.

Again, does anybody do this?
Actually, there's a waiting list.

The latest data from the US Citizenship and Immigration Service indicates that at the end of 2016 there were over 20,000 applications pending for this class of visa.

Are you doing the math here? That represents as much as $20 billion dollars and 200,000 jobs.

Pending.

Between 2008 and 2016, there were 33,536 visas granted in this category. I'll do the math for you: $33.5 billion invested (Plus all the application fees, which are high) and 335,000 jobs.

Just sayin'.

## All the Americans hate immigrants!

This is another stereotype that drives me nuts. It is just so untrue, and unfair.

Yes, there are "hate groups." And they are getting a lot of publicity at the moment. And even worse, some are feeling enabled and justified these days. So they are even more likely to say something mean.

But for every one of "those" people, I believe there are dozens, hundreds, thousands, MILLIONS of people who do NOT feel that way.

The vast number of Americans want peace and to help people.

Have you seen these signs cropping up everywhere?

In the office building where I work, we have a sign at the front from the #AllAreWelcome movement.

**PEOPLE OF COLOR**
**IMMIGRANTS**
**REFUGEES**
**MUSLIMS**
**WOMEN**
**LGBTQ**
**YOU**
**US**

**ALL ARE WELCOME HERE**
#ALLAREWELCOME

I know, Americans are by no means unique in their willingness to help other people. The United Nations is made up of many countries who are contributing to good work around the world. But it is undeniable that Americans STEP UP more than any other country. You will find our missionaries doing famine relief, our engineers on the scene for flood and earthquake recovery, and our scientists (if not our politicians) on the forefront of environmental preservation.

Within our own borders, does any other country in the world have so many charities, churches, or nonprofits that are out helping communities? In other countries, how often would you see the members of a "blessed" (meaning affluent) church creating missions to help those less fortunate across the world, or even in the same city?

In Spring 2016, the Pew Research Center asked people around the world: "Do you think having an increasing number of people of different races, ethnic groups, and nationalities in our country makes it a better place to live or a worse place to live?"

Just 8 percent of Americans said such immigration makes the country a "worse place to live," compared to 34 percent of Europeans. (*http://bit.ly/BWStats4)*

The misperception that Americans are not welcoming of immigrants creates needless conflict. When I see school principals, nurses, first responders, pastors, and nonprofit groups trying so desperately to help everyone and anyone, it frustrates me to hear immigrants and their supporters say, "They all hate us," or "We have to UNITE to FIGHT!"

How is that true unity?

I don't believe fighting is the answer. In fact, like many, I believe that fighting just leads to more fighting.

Rather, let's focus on the communities, organizations, and influencers who are doing GOOD.

Later in this book, I'll talk to you about a wonderful woman named Jocelyn Miller. Jocelyn is an African American woman who started an educational resource center in honor of her late father, and she welcomes people from all races, religions, and communities.

Let's build up people like Jocelyn. Let's support them, and get THEM on the evening news.

## 4.1 IT'S TIME TO STOP WASTING TALENT.

So, what about the idea that all the immigrants are poor farm workers?

At The ShareLingo Project, we see a lot of immigrants in our English/Spanish conversation classes. We like to learn more about each other, so we ask what they do, and often we get responses like:

- "In Mexico, I was a systems analyst."

- "In Bolivia, I was a lawyer."

- "In Peru, I was a musician."

When we hear this, we encourage the people to change their thinking, and to say, "I AM a systems analyst. I AM a lawyer. I AM a musician." Moving to this country doesn't change what they are any more than me moving to Costa Rica would make me not an engineer.

Unfortunately, being able to WORK in one's profession is often another matter. (I mentioned this problem in the previous chapter when I spoke about the Spring Institute.) There are far too many professionals here in the U.S. (indeed, around the world—have you seen what is happening in Europe?) who are working in very basic jobs rather than in their professions. I believe that this is a terrible waste of talent.

In one of our ShareLingo classes here in Denver, I met Maria, a systems analyst who came to the United States from Mexico. When Maria moved here, she got a job cleaning hotels.

One day, while making up a room, the guest at the hotel asked Maria for a pillow.

She didn't know what a pillow was.

But the woman just kept saying, louder and louder, pillow, Pillow, PILLOW!

The closest word Maria had in her vocabulary was "pelo" (hair). So, not knowing what else to do, she brought the guest a hair brush.

That didn't go well—for Maria, the guest, or the hotel. The woman just yelled at her more.

Clearly, Maria is intelligent, but the guest, because of her frustration, made Maria feel inadequate. Maria said she cried. A lot. She wanted to help that guest. And she didn't want to lose her job.

It gave her incentive to study hard, learn English, and get out of the hotel and back to her profession.

But for some people, that's not possible. Simply learning English is not enough.

After ten years living here in the United States, Belén, a lawyer from Peru, still works the deli counter at Safeway. Belén's story is a little different than Maria's. Like Maria, Belén has worked hard to learn more English. Her kids, all now grown and living here also as citizens, are fluent in both English and Spanish, and Belén was just blessed with her first granddaughter, so she couldn't be happier in that regard.

But she knows that it is very unlikely she will ever become a lawyer here in the U.S. Belén is passionate about lots of causes, but can't use her talents to address them.

The time and expense needed for her to be able to practice law in this country are just beyond her means. I think it's a shame she couldn't find work in the legal field, in spite of the enormous need for trained bilingual lawyers here in our country that understand the problems and can work with the immigrant communities.

Think about it. Suppose you are a doctor, engineer, accountant, systems analyst, nurse, or teacher. Whatever it is, you're good at it. You've invested years getting your education. Now, suppose that, for some reason, you decide (or are compelled) to move to a different country. Maybe it's to be with family, or for health reasons, or your government is corrupt—whatever the reason, you move. And when you get to your new country, where you have such high hopes, you find that due to lack of language skills, or because your credentials are not recognized, you can't get a job within your profession.

What would you do? Would you work in a deli? Would you clean hotels or people's houses?

I am happy that, partly with the help of The ShareLingo Project, Maria and Belén now speak English and are able to tell these stories.

To put another perspective on this idea, suppose your company hires a $100,000-a-year civil engineer from Chile to do a $20,000-a-year cleaning job. In my mind, that's an $80,000-a-year waste of talent, not to mention lost productivity and tax revenue.

I hope you will agree that we, as a society, MUST help immigrants learn English, and ALSO give them an affordable path to work within their professions.

Do you have a story like Maria or Belén?

Did you or your parents or someone you know set aside a profession when you or they came here?

Or, if you're from here, have you been to another country and tried to work in a professional job?

Did you speak the language of that country?

Please join the discussion. Visit the website below to tell us your story.

*http://bit.ly/BWFeedback1*

## 4.2 HOW DO YOU FEEL ABOUT U.S. WORKERS SENDING MONEY TO MEXICO OR CHINA?

I was reading the Daily Mail recently. That's a British news source. In it, I read an article saying that citizens (citizens, mind you!) in the USA are sending $120 billion a year to their families "back home." The article said that more than $23 billion is sent to Mexico, $13 billion to China, and over $10 billion each to India and the Philippines.

Hold that thought.

The Daily Mail made the situation sound terrible. There has been a lot of talk about this "drain" on American resources. "They shouldn't be allowed to send all that money to Mexico!" Or, you know, "They're taking American jobs!"

I disagree.

First, if we didn't need the workers, they wouldn't be here working. Period. (See Chapter 6 for the story about Metco

Landscaping, which brings nearly 300 seasonal workers from Mexico to Denver each year.) The premise of "A Day Without a Mexican" is pretty true here in Denver, where Spanish speakers are in every corner of our community, filling all kinds of jobs. Yes, they are commonly the cooks, cleaners, roofers, construction workers, and even garbage collectors. But they are also security guards, accountants, salespeople, executives and business owners.

Now—here's the point. The people sending money back to their families are the ones who have jobs—the ones who are helping to build our economy.

If someone is earning a living and wants to send money to their family, isn't that a good thing?

> After I got out of college and got a job, I sent money to my Grandmother for many years—right up until she died. My Grandma lived in Iowa, so that's OK, right? But my heritage is English (British) and Czechoslovakian (I know ... immigrants, right?) and if she had been in one of those countries, I guess I may have been sending money to her there.

So, if someone is sending money to their mom in Mexico, or even China (Oh my!!), why is that bad?

At The ShareLingo Project, we see a lot of immigrants who want to learn English. In our classes, people become friends and build a trust between each other. So we get to ask questions—personal questions—and get real answers from the heart.

Guess what—a lot of them have jobs. In fact, a lot of them have two or three jobs. There are a lot of immigrant workers in this country who work a second or third job JUST so they can send money back home. (Would you do that?) They consider it a responsibility, an obligation, and more importantly, a privilege.

I wish, I wish, I wish, that more native-born Americans felt like this.

*Source—http://bit.ly/BWStats5*

# 5.0 Do Immigrants Even Want to Learn English?

*"In the long history of humankind (and animal kind, too) those who learned to collaborate and improvise most effectively have prevailed."*
— **Charles Darwin**

**"You're in America. Speak English!"**

Why do people say this?

No, really, I want to know. *Why?*

**If you were in Paris
visiting the Eiffel Tower,
and you called your MOM—
would you talk to her in French?**

If someone is speaking in another language, it doesn't necessarily mean that they don't speak English. It just means that they CAN speak another language.

Last night, a good friend of mine was talking to her Mom. In Cantonese. Someone passing by said something stupid: "You're in America. Speak English." See the irony? He's talking to someone in English telling them to learn English. If she was speaking in Cantonese, shouldn't he have said that in Cantonese?

Anyway, this friend of mine is SUPER smart. She went to the University of Denver, which is a prestigious school. She majored in marketing, and now she's a PR and marketing GURU.

**She speaks English perfectly.**

She just happened to be talking to her Mom.

So, **to the people who say, "You're in America. Speak English,"** I have something to say—

**I want your help.**

That's probably not what you expected.

Maybe you expected me to say something mean, like:

> "If you don't speak Cherokee, or Navajo, or one of the other 144 languages that Indigenous People still speak in this country, meaning, you're not Native American, then you need to go back to wherever your ancestors came from."

But that's not what I'm saying.

## Dear Mr./Mrs. "You're in America. Speak English," I need your help.

I think we have some common ground. Because like you, I believe that everyone in America should have an opportunity to speak English. So they can easily talk to their doctors, the police, and their children's teachers. So they can understand our culture. So they can make and buy our products and services.

That's where you come in.

Since there is no magic pill to learn English, they need someone to practice with.

That's you.

I'm asking you to come and help someone practice English. Simple. I'll provide the materials. I'll teach you how to teach them.

As a bonus, if you want to learn Spanish at the same time, an immigrant can teach you, and I can help with that too. You can learn more about other cultures. Learn more about the world.

You can be *smarter*. Did you know that people who speak more than one language are literally smarter than people who only speak one? That's because speaking a second language changes your brain. It creates more synapses—those connections inside your brain that help you think and remember. You can think about problems in more than one way.

But even if you don't want that—even if you don't want to know another language, or know more about other cultures, or know more about the world—even if you don't want to help ME—even if you choose ignorance over education—that's OKAY, because there is another option you can do instead.

You can go down to any community center, school, nonprofit, or church that has an ESL program—ESL is "English as a Second Language"—and you can volunteer to help someone practice English.

If you truly believe that everyone in America should be able to speak English, it would be great if you actually help them do that.

But know this, when you teach them, you will get to know them as people. You will probably become friends with them.

And you may find yourself saying,

"Welcome to America. I can help you you learn English."

And you may find yourself thinking,

*You're in America.*

    *Speak English.*

        *. . . Any Language You Want.*

**ESL classes are packed.**

When I was learning Spanish, I volunteered to teach English to ESL students. As I said in the previous section, ESL stands for "English as a Second Language." These classes started me thinking about creating the ShareLingo model.

Way back then, I was certainly not the only person teaching an ESL class. They were all over the place—in churches, community centers, and even community colleges—and they were very well-attended.

Even now, on most Tuesday and Wednesday evenings, you will find me teaching classes at my church—pro bono.

As I said in the previous section, I think everyone should have an opportunity to learn English if they want to. **So, do they want to?**

*YES.*

Now more than ever, the immigrants WANT to speak English. They have many reasons.

Consider this:

When I am out and about, I ask lots of people one simple question:

"Do you speak Spanish?"

The overwhelming response is: "I Wish."

You may be one of these people!

If there was a magic pill that I could give to people to teach them Spanish, I think a lot of people would pay $1,000 or more just for that pill. But there isn't a pill.

To learn a new language, you have to study. And practice.

It's generally not URGENT for Anglos to learn Spanish. And if it is urgent, it may not be CRITICAL.

Many school teachers desperately want to bridge the achievement gap. That's urgent, I would say. And that may make learning a little Spanish urgent too. But it's not critical. Teachers still teach, even if they can't communicate with their students' parents.

But let's look at immigrants.

Is learning English unimportant, important, urgent, or critical?

Yes, it is very possible to live in the U.S. and not speak English. Say you speak Chinese. Can you find a community to live in, food to buy, and some sort of job? Yes.

And if you speak Spanish, it's even easier. There are Spanish speakers everywhere, and Spanish-speaking markets, accountants, bankers, television, and car repair
places.

So, you may think that for Spanish speakers, speaking English is unimportant.

I want to share a story that one of our ShareLingo facilitators wrote. She wrote it in Spanish, because she's speaking to the Hispanic community. But she is fully bilingual, with almost zero accent.

# MARA'S STORY

The original Spanish has been provided in the appendices.

## Uniting Communities
## Breaking Barriers

It is often heard that "America is the land of opportunity, and that if you are willing to work hard, you will achieve your dreams." But what is not talked about, and that has a great impact on our path to success, is the importance of integrating into a new culture. From the food and the language to the way we spend our free time are different from in our country of origin. I am Mexican, and although there are many Mexicans in the state of Colorado, the culture shock I experienced when I arrived in this country was very big and intimidating.

However, if you have emigrated to the United States in search of the long-awaited "American Dream," you have probably noticed how our immigrant community tends to isolate itself from American culture.

I still remember the terror I had in having to go to an American supermarket, where, of course, people did not speak Spanish. And the frustration at the feeling that I could not order at a fast food restaurant. The language barrier was huge. So, in order to not feel helpless, I did everything I needed to in Spanish. Luckily, finding super markets and Latino restaurants here in Denver is quite easy.

Time was passing, and little by little, I realized that, although one, yes, can survive in this country without speaking the language, the loss of not being involved in American culture is enough and irreversible, from meeting new people, making a phone call, attending a conference, or listening to the music of the moment, to talking to my teachers. All this helped me to understand that, in order to reach the "American Dream," I needed to be included in the culture, and of course, to master English.

Once I decided to focus on and learn English the best I could, I noticed that my list of options expanded. As well as going to any super market, cinema, restaurant, or church, even my way of thinking expanded little by little. Now I have the opportunity to experience all these activities without the barrier of not knowing how to communicate in another language. I no longer feel afraid to order a hamburger with fries, just like I feel able to go to a bank and make a transaction. On the contrary, learning English has increased my level of confidence in myself. And it has given me the security to feel that I also belong to this country like any other person.

The ShareLingo Project exists because they want our immigrant community to take advantage of all the opportunities that exist in this country. Let's stop excluding and segregating ourselves. The mission of ShareLingo is that the Anglo and Latino communities unite through the language. That the Americans learn

Spanish, as well as that the Latinos learn English. They will also benefit by learning our language, and their list of options and opportunities will likewise expand.

Can you imagine how wonderful it would be to see more Americans interested in our culture, buying fresh cheese in Latino super markets, or going to the movies in Spanish?

From Mara's story, you can see that it's certainly _not_ unimportant.

Now, let's look at something else.

## Citizenship

According to the U.S. Citizenship and Immigration Services, more than 6.6 million people were naturalized as U.S. citizens during the last decade.

But did you know that there are lots of permanent residents here (yes, LEGALLY) who qualify for citizenship but haven't taken the test because it's in English? You can study for it in almost any language, but you have to do the test, and the interview, in English.

According to the Department of Homeland Security, as of 2013 (the latest data available) there was an estimated 13.1 million legal permanent residents, of which, an estimated 8.8 million were eligible to naturalize.

Do we all agree, based on both past and present political climates, that any path to citizenship will probably include an English proficiency component?

Do you think that, for them, speaking English is urgent?

I would argue that it makes it critical.

The truth is, ESL classes are packed. All over this country. In churches, community centers, libraries, and nonprofits, it is common to see classes of 10, 20, 30 people.

In my church in Colorado where I volunteer, nearly 100 ESL students make up eight ESL classes every Tuesday and Wednesday evening.

So, yes-

The vast majority of immigrants DO want to speak English.

# 6.0 Sector/Industry Examples

*"In the long history of humankind (and animal kind, too) those who learned to collaborate and improvise most effectively have prevailed."*
**—Charles Darwin**

As I stated in Chapter 2—"Who is this Book for?"—not all of the examples in this chapter will apply to YOU, though I hope that you might find one, two, or more that apply. My goal is to illustrate that nearly every sector can benefit from helping people connect across languages and cultures. And there are many motivations for learning another language—for job, for mission, or to find love!

No matter the sector you are in, people come together every day to work toward a common goal. Yes, some are there just for the paycheck, and that's perfectly OK. But most want to feel that they are coming together to achieve something bigger than they can achieve by themselves.

Yet ... only a third of U.S. workers say they are engaged in their work, according to a recent Gallup survey. And half of the workforce is looking for a different job. A lot of that has to do with a feeling that they are not engaged in a higher purpose.

Language barriers are partly to blame in many industries. Employees who do not speak the same language do not gel. Customers AND employees get a bad taste in their mouth after a flubbed service experience caused by a language misunderstanding. Health care and safety net workers feel powerless when critical information doesn't come through cleanly.

As Darwin says above, collaboration will help you prevail.

The word "industry" is used loosely. You may not feel that "government" is an industry, for example, but it is a "sector" of our economy.

Also, the sections of this chapter are not meant to represent any sort of order of importance. If they did, I would have put education first, because I'm most passionate about that. But is it more important than "health" or "government?" That's debatable.

Regardless of where YOUR sector falls in the list, know that I think what YOU are doing is IMPORTANT.

I applaud you, and thank you, for having gotten this far in the book, and for being interested in helping YOUR industry or YOUR community break down cultural barriers.

## 6.1 HOSPITALITY

If you work in the hospitality industry—that may be hotel, restaurant, convention center, resort, transportation, etc.—you are probably seeing a much more diverse clientele, and a much more diverse workforce. If you work in hospitality and are reading this book, your property or organization is probably experiencing language and cultural disconnects.

Earlier I told you about Maria, a systems analyst who worked in a hotel when she first came to the United States and who brought a hairbrush to a guest who had asked for a pillow. Now, I want to share another hospitality-related story.

## Jennifer and David / Ana and Judith

Like many areas of our community, immigrants make up a large part of the service staff in the hospitality industry.

Steve, a friend of mine who's a front desk manager at a major hotel brand, lamented to me one day how frustrating it can be when an angry guest calls up at 6 p.m., saying they just got back from a day of meetings and their room isn't cleaned.

The guest says, "The maid knocked on the door this morning while I was getting dressed and I asked her to come back later. She said OK."

So now, the guest is frustrated, and so is the manager. The manager gets on the phone and calls the head of housekeeping—one of the few bilingual people in the building. That person finds a maid (not many working at that time of day) and sends her to the room. Just the communication process, from person to person, can take 10 or 15 minutes.

And of course, by this time, the damage is done. The guest has had a bad experience. Nobody is happy, <u>including the maid</u>. She wants to help. She wants to do a good job. She doesn't want to lose her job! She just didn't understand when the guest said, "Come back later." All she understood was that the guest didn't want the room cleaned (at that time).

What can we do?

Jennifer and David are front of house.

Ana and Judith (pronounced Who'd-EET) are in housekeeping.

Jennifer and Ana, along with eight other people, are doing classes in the hotel once a week to teach each other English and Spanish (The ShareLingo model). The materials they use cover not only the common basic lessons—greetings, colors, numbers, etc.—but also hotel-specific vocabulary and phrases.

- What time is breakfast?

- I need fresh towels, more blankets, shampoo...

- <u>Can you come back and clean later?</u>

So, after a week or two, Jennifer and David are walking down a hallway and they pass Ana and Judith.

In the past, they may, at most, have nodded heads, or offered some other very cursory greeting.

More likely, Judith and Ana would have moved over to the side of the hallway and simply waited for Jennifer and David to pass by. Sad, right?

But NOW what happens?

Jennifer and Ana see each other—and they don't ignore each other.

> JENNIFER: "Hola, Ana! ¿Como estás?" [Hello Ana, How are you?]
>
> ANA: "Good morning, Ms. Jennifer! Bien, tú?" [I'm well, you?]
>
> JENNIFER: "Bien, bien. ¿Cómo amaneciste?" [Very well. How was your morning?]
>
> ANA: "Phew. Busy, busy!!"
>
> JENNIFER: "Jajaja, como siempre!" [Haha, like always!]
>
> ANA: "Qué tengas un lindo día, Ms. Jennifer." [Have a beautiful day, Ms. Jennifer.]
>
> JENNIFER: "Igualmente, Ana." [You too, Ana.]

David looks at Jennifer—his mouth is hanging open. He taps her on the arm. "You speak Spanish?"

> Jennifer: "Actually, I'm learning Spanish, here in the hotel. Ana is one of the people teaching me. Did you know that in Venezuela she was a nurse? That country is a mess right now. The government took

away everything from her family. They came here as refugees."

David: "Wow! That's terrible. My sister is a nurse. She had to work really hard. Why's Ana working in a hotel?"

Jennifer: "Her credentials aren't recognized here. And she needs to speak more English. She's working on that. But for now, she has to help feed her family. Did you know she's never had a sick day here?"

David hears something more.

**Ana is *smart*. Ana has *value*. Ana is *nice*. Ana has *dreams* and *ambitions*. Ana is *reliable*.**

On the other side, Judith stops Ana and HER mouth is hanging open, and SHE says, "¿Cómo conoces a Ms. Jennifer?" [How do you know Ms. Jennifer?]

"Ella me enseña inglés en las clases. Está aprendiendo español."
[She teaches me English in the classes. She's learning Spanish.]

So Judith hears,

**Jennifer *doesn't* hate us. Jennifer is *nice*. Jennifer is *patient*. And she may also think, Jennifer is *someone I can go to* for help.**

Now, not only does Ana know what, "Can you come back later?" means, but Jennifer knows how to say, in Spanish, "Mr. Jones in room 227 needs his room cleaned."

She has the confidence to pick up the phone and talk directly to Ana. So if Mr Jones in 227 needs something, it can be handled directly—in just a minute or two—saving the 10 or 15 minutes that it previously took to run everything through the few bilingual people on site.

Imagine this program working in your property.

What are the benefits?
- Communication
- Efficiency
- Staff Retention
- Guest Satisfaction

There is a ripple effect. Not only Jennifer and Ana, but also David and Judith gained some cultural insight.

Maybe David stops to have a second thought about that stereotype that, "All the immigrants are poor farm workers, draining our economy."

And Judith may have second thoughts about, "All the Americans hate us."

As I mentioned at the beginning, the "hospitality industry" doesn't just include hotels. For example:
- In Restaurants—whether you're a franchise owner for McDonalds, or head chef of your own place,

wouldn't you like better communication, efficiency, staff retention, and guest satisfaction?

- If you manage a conference and exhibition center—isn't staff training and retention your BIGGEST headache?

- What about airports?

- Taxi, transportation, and parking companies?

- Resorts? Golf courses?

All of these have links to "hospitality."

Keep in mind, Spanish speakers don't just make up the labor pool.

More and more, they are your guests and visitors.

Follow the ShareLingo roadmap in the next chapter to help you implement a cross-cultural language class that can really help your staff understand each other.

If you need any help, or you're just too busy to develop this kind of class yourself, please reach out to us.

## 6.2 CONSTRUCTION AND LANDSCAPING

The trades.

Builders. Roofers. Contractors. From painting and drywall to framing and, more and more, plumbing and electrical. Latinos are making up an increasing percentage of the labor pool in all of these areas. They know the business end of a shovel, they work hard, and they don't whine.

Company owner William meets foreman James on a construction site. As they walk, they talk:

James: "Hey, Boss."

William: "Hey, James—how we doin'?"

James: "On time and on budget."

William: "MAN! Words I needed to hear. The job downtown is driving me crazy. You guys are doing great."

*Man drives past on a skid steer (Bobcat).*

James: "Hold on-" Then he yells, "Marco!" at the man passing by.

Marco, stopping the skid steer: "Yes, Mister James!"

James: "Ve al lado de la oficina, por favor. Necesitamos más arena para el cemento. Dónde está Héctor?"

[Go over by the office, please. We need more sand for the cement. Where's Hector?]

Marco: "OK, no problem, Mr. James! I'll go get the sand. Héctor está allá!" *(points...)*

*Marcos heads off.*

William: "Who's that? And wait—you speak Spanish? Since when?!"

James, smiling: "William, that's Marco—your best guy. He gets here early, leaves late, never misses a day, never complains." *(Nods at another man.)* "And that's Jesus, that's Hector, and Roberto is here someplace too. Really fun guys. You should get to know them."

William: "What?!—How'd you do this?"

James: "OK. Me, Greg, Bill, Steve, and Andrea from accounting—we get together twice a week here after work with Marco and his crew. They help us learn Spanish, and we help them learn English.

"It's called ShareLingo, and trust me, it's about the coolest thing I've ever done."

"William, I told you about this—you approved it. You're even paying for it!"

William: "Really—Spanish classes. Twice a week. Expensive?"

James: "I know it sounds like a cost—but it helps the bottom line. It's not just Spanish. It's Spanish and English. It's helped our production, our safety, and morale. Guys are sticking around longer. Nobody has left since we started the program. You know what it costs to find and train a new guy. And like I said, we're on time and on budget. That's because the whole team is working better together.

"The cool thing is we're getting to know Marco and the crew—as people. And they're getting to know us. Before this, everyone used to stay separate. Like, on breaks—they would go one way, we'd go the other. Now, most of the time, we even eat lunch together so we can practice more. We laugh and joke around. They're funny guys! And if something comes up, we handle it together. If they have a question, they ask me. They don't just guess—so, less misunderstandings and mistakes."

Working with a mixture of people who speak different languages and come from different cultures isn't all bliss and happiness, is it?

If you are in this field, you have probably noticed a cultural reality.

Latinos generally don't ever say, "No, Boss." And they rarely, if ever, say, "Sorry, I don't understand."

Why is that?

> You say, "Plant that tree on the left side of the sidewalk, 10 feet from the corner."
>
> Worker says, "OK, Boss."
>
> You come back four hours later, and the tree is planted, but it isn't even close to where you said. What happened? Is the worker stupid? Or was there a misunderstanding?
>
> Were you facing North or South when you said "left"? Which "corner" were you referring to?
>
> Maybe he planted the tree on the left side from HIS perspective. And maybe it's 10 feet from the corner of a building, not the corner of the street.

So, you say, "If you didn't understand, why didn't you ASK me?"

He can't do that—yet.

Let me explain a cultural difference.

The Latino culture has experienced about 600 years of what is fundamentally slavery. I know, actual slavery was outlawed many many years ago. But even to this day, the worker-boss dynamic is steeped in an inter-cultural history that looks a lot like slavery. For Latinos, questioning authority is simply not culturally permitted. It's not OKAY to question your boss.

But here in the U.S., we WANT someone to ask questions. We EXPECT someone to ask for clarification, and when it doesn't happen, we resort to tongue-lashings and ostracism—metaphorical whips and chains.

So, two things need to happen:

1. We need to show our immigrant labor pool that it's OKAY to ask questions, and that they can trust us.

2. We need to understand that even if an immigrant says they understand—"OK, Boss."—they may not. It's best to make sure you are being clear.

How can you kill both those birds with the one stone?

Have the English and Spanish speakers teach each other. Have them focus not only on the general words and phrases like, "Good morning," but also on your industry specifics.

The extra benefit you will gain from this is a connection and trust between the cultures. Not only will Juan know how to say, "I don't understand," in English, he will also have the trust in you to be able to actually say that to your face without fearing reprisal.

Other cultural matters may include how to dress appropriately for the job or important safety precautions.

> Juan, you have to wear a hard hat and safety goggles. If you lose them or break them, we will give you new ones. That doesn't make you less macho—it keeps you from getting hurt so we don't have to find and train someone else, and it also keeps our insurance rates down.

The thing to remember is, what may seem obvious to you is absolutely not obvious to someone speaking a different language and who has had different cultural experiences.

Say they are doing your concrete work. Chances are, in their country, concrete was 100 percent mixed and poured by hand. In five-gallon buckets. Workers carry or pass the buckets from hand to hand up to whatever level it needs to be, and then another worker pours it into the form.

If something breaks, they make do. They work around it. They don't stop and wait around for a new—whatever.

So here, if something breaks, or it starts to rain, or there aren't exactly the right tools, or they don't have their safety glasses on, they do the job anyway.

Implementing programs to improve communication and safety SAVE you money.

How?

Let's talk about METCO for a minute.

## METCO LANDSCAPING

Metco Landscaping is a $50 million-a-year business (And may hit $60 Million this year). That's pretty impressive for a company that basically installs grass and sprinkler systems. It's even more impressive when you consider that here in Colorado, there are several months a year when they can't do anything. They do almost all that business during the growing season from March to September.

Every year, Metco brings nearly 300 H2B immigrants to Denver from Mexico. Why? Because they HAVE to. It's not cheap. They have to apply and pay for the visas. They have to send people down to Mexico to bring the workers here. They have to rent buses, pay for food, and document EVERYTHING.

But they can't do the work or make that kind of money without workers. Simple as that.

Do you think they would hire locally if they could? Absolutely. And they are constantly looking for that competitive advantage so that local workers want to work with them. So the language program they adopted— ShareLingo—does double duty: it helps their Spanish-speaking workforce do their jobs more safely and efficiently, AND it gives their local English-speaking managers a free perk. They have a goal for their management to be 85 percent bilingual within the next three years.

A custom curriculum was created for Metco to help their English and Spanish speakers teach each other. General phrases, like how to say, "Good Morning" were included. But it also included a lot of industry-specific information—like what different "locate" colors mean ("Locates" are those marks that are painted on the ground before digging— red = electricity, yellow = gas, blue = fresh water, etc.) and lots of safety information.

According to Greg Ritcher, their director of training, these programs have helped them work with their insurance company to reduce annual insurance costs by as much as $58,000. The insurance savings alone are a 7X return on their ShareLingo investment.

What about "soft" costs? Those things you can't measure directly. What about the participants? Do they see any value?

Every morning, very early, an army of workers arrives at the business. Hundreds of trucks and crews go out to get the jobs done. But before that, there are meetings and briefings. And something else—every morning, the whole team does stretching exercises to keep people from being injured. They have set up a routine so that as this army is doing their morning stretching and exercises, every person learns just a little more English or Spanish. They swap words or phrases of the day.

Fundamentally, Metco does this because they care about people. But believe me, they are very aware that these programs have positive effects on the bottom line.

Sticky Notes: It's hard to even describe how effective this program is for building trust—so here is a picture illustrating that aspect. In this image, the participants, both English and Spanish speakers, were learning body parts as part of a lesson on Safety. "My shoulder hurts," for example. Someone in the group had the bright idea to write body parts on sticky notes and stick them to each other! And it worked. Not only were they really learning body parts, they were building a real bond with each other. How much trust does it take to let someone stick a piece of paper to your cheek, ear, and nose? And to feel comfortable doing the same thing to them?

## 6.3 HEALTHCARE

If you are in healthcare, you probably are seeing a lot more diversity in your patients. And you are probably experiencing more difficulty helping them because of language and cultural differences.

Doctors, nurses, dentists, nursing homes, paramedics, and other first responders are all seeing this, and it's stressing the industry's administrators and HR professionals.

> Even though we naturally think about problems we face when the PATIENTS do not speak English, we can't forget that lots of support staff in these professions may not speak English, or not speak it well.

People who work in healthcare are not bad people, right? You're not a bad person, right? In fact, you're some of the BEST people, right? So why are so many worried about being sued? Why are so many being chastised? Why are so many unhappy?

Like teachers, many of you are overworked and underpaid. You're doing this because it's your calling. Anything that just makes it more difficult takes away the luster, right?

The Hippocratic Oath, although evolving over time, remains the most ancient and lasting testament to a physician's commitment to do good. (*http://bit.ly/BWResource5*)

But when there is a disconnect, whether due to language or cultural misunderstandings, the best of care cannot be provided. Maybe you don't feel like you're doing everything you can for the patient.

This book is about bringing people together through language, so I won't dwell on all the other aspects of good healthcare. But I acknowledge, gratefully, what you do for our communities every day.

Are hospitals and healthcare providers required to provide translation services?

In many cases, yes. Those of you in the industry know there are a web of federal and state regulations that aim to ensure equal access. Often, the rules prescribe translation services. And when they don't, you know that meeting patients where they are just makes practical and moral sense.

You want the best for your patients, right?

How would you feel if YOU couldn't explain YOUR symptoms to your doctor or paramedics?

One of the most famous cases in history is still a poignant reminder of the importance of language and cultural understanding.

WAY back on Jan. 22, 1980, Willie Ramirez, an 18-

year-old high school athlete in Florida, ended up a quadriplegic due to language and cultural misunderstandings. Willie spent two days in an ER before a neurological consult determined that he had a brain aneurysm. Ultimately, this led to a $71 million lawsuit against the hospital.

Prior to arriving at the hospital by ambulance in a comatose state, he stated that he was feeling "intoxicado." In Cuban Spanish, this simply means "sick" or "nauseous." Because intoxicado and intoxicated are false cognates (words that sound the same but have different meanings), the doctor misunderstood Willie's condition to be related to drugs or alcohol.

Complicating the matter, the doctor did not know the cultural tendency for Latinos to avoid contradicting people in authority. So, even though Willie's family did not agree with what the doctor was saying and tried to say he did not drink alcohol, they could not INSIST that the doctor look at other options.

Willy's case is historic. That's why it is still being talked about today. But there are thousands of lesser and more current cases involving aspects some may not even consider.

Health literacy is a huge problem even among English speakers—I once saw a doctor's jaw drop when her longtime patient said he thought his "hypertension" medicine was to treat "hyperactivity."

But the health literacy problem is compounded for the non-English speaker who receives a prescription from the doctor and fills it at the hospital pharmacy. The chances are pretty good that, along with the prescription, they will receive several pages of printed information, instructions, and warnings about the medication—all in English.

When asked if they understand (ASSUMING they are asked), they may nod and say, "Yes." But they don't necessarily understand. Culturally, they don't feel comfortable asking questions, and may think they will get a friend or family member to translate at a later time. And maybe they just thought you were asking if they would take the medicine at all, so they say, "Yes."

So there is a misunderstanding. And that can lead to complications—costly, life-or-death complications.

If someone has a problem, there are plenty of lawyers anxious to bring a case against you.

And the last thing you need is to lose a lawsuit, which could cost you (or your institution) vastly more than translation services.

But again, that's not the point. The language/culture issue shouldn't be just about avoiding liability.

Isn't it about the patient?

Well, the American Hospital Association thinks so. In 2015, the AHA launched its #123forEquity pledge campaign. According to its web site:

It builds on the efforts of the National Call to Action to Eliminate Healthcare Disparities—a joint effort of the AHA, American College of Healthcare Executives, Association of American Medical Colleges, Catholic Health Association of the United States, and America's Essential Hospitals—and asks hospital and health system leaders to begin taking action to accelerate progress on the following areas:

- Increasing the collection and use of race, ethnicity, **language preference,** and other socio-demographic data

- Increasing cultural competency training

- Increasing diversity in leadership and governance

Hospitals all over the country are signing this pledge and doing their utmost to provide, among other things, translation services for non-English speakers.

*http://bit.ly/BWResource6*

*http://bit.ly/BWResource7*

While there are many options for translation—ranging from bilingual staff, to telephone translation, and even, unfortunately, having bilingual family members, including children—translate (which is NOT recommended), these options fail to address some very important factors.

According to an article published in the **Annals of Emergency Medicine**, non-professional interpreters (such as staff or family members) produced as much as a 22 percent error rate in a clinical environment as opposed to just a 2 percent error rate using experienced professional interpreters. Of the nearly 1,900 errors noted during the study, about 18 percent could have had serious clinical consequences.

I spoke with Olga Garcia, a manager at Denver Health, which is an extremely important healthcare provider in the Denver community.

One of the things that Olga highlighted in our conversation was the fact that immigrants, documented or not, are scared right now. So they avoid any setting in which they may be identified or cataloged. This means that, often, they have waited until something has gotten more serious than if it had been treated early. About 25 percent of Denver Health patients speak Spanish, and they also deal with dozens of other languages. Whenever possible, they hire or train bilingual staff. When that's not possible (if they don't have someone working who speaks Hindi for example), they do use translation services.

Claudia Escobedo, a patient navigator for Denver Hospice, is a native Spanish speaker and is working on her English skills through ShareLingo. She wishes more of her colleagues could fully understand their Spanish-speaking patients. "There are times when they have diagnosed a patient with dementia because they are not following doctor's orders. But really, they just don't understand the language. They might be labeled an 'aggressive' patient because they push their caregivers away. But really, they don't know why someone is touching them. It's language and it's culture."

How can you help educate the immigrant community about healthcare?

How can you help educate healthcare professionals about immigrant needs?

Do both at once. Kill two birds with one stone.

Welcome the immigrant community into your space—your hospital, clinic, or nursing home—to meet, face-to-face, with staff who have a desire to learn Spanish (or another language).

At the same time that both sides are learning about the language *(How do you say, "Pain in my chest?")*, they will also have an opportunity to discuss programs and services that are available.

> We can teach them, for example, that they can make doctor's appointments and they don't have to go to the emergency room for every little thing.

> We can also teach them that it is OKAY, and EXPECTED, for them to ask questions if they do not fully understand everything.

These groups, although created for the purpose of sharing language, also educate both sides about important cultural differences. And they will build trust and understanding.

Please, join the effort to help connect the English- and Spanish-speaking communities, and to make a difference in healthcare.

One of ShareLingo's first pilot programs was done at Kaiser Permanente* here in Denver. We invited Spanish speakers to come into a Kaiser hospital to work with the English-speaking marketing staff. This was when the Affordable Care Act was just coming out, and they had a real desire to learn more Spanish. You can see a news story about this class here: *http://bit.ly/BWVideo7*

ShareLingo takes learning a language to the next level with one-on-one practice with native speakers.

Healthcare, in all its forms, is on the "front lines" when it comes to the interaction of different cultures. YOU are on the front line. People get sick and have accidents, no matter their race, religion, economic status, or sexual orientation.

Thank you!

*Kaiser Permanente has an OUTSTANDING commitment to understanding and treating people in spite of language and cultural differences. They hire diverse medical personnel, tailor care to be ethnically appropriate, and are attuned to the influence culture has on health. Their programs are proactive. They are constantly seeking to better understand their communities and what their needs are.*

## 6.4 EDUCATION

*I have cherished the ideal of a democratic and free society in which all persons live together in harmony and with equal opportunities.*
*~ Nelson Mandela*

First of all, if you are in education at any level, OMG—You guys ROCK! I wish, I WISH we as a society didn't make your jobs so hard. But thank YOU for your passion, commitment, and contribution.

I'm sure I don't need to tell you about the achievement gap—the unconscionable difference in performance between minority students and white students. I know you must tear your hair out when you see the difference in reading, writing, and math scores, and that you are working each school year to close the gap.

Of course, the issue is complicated, and many factors can contribute to the achievement gap.

One contributing factor that has been identified by numerous studies relates to "Parental (or Family) Engagement." Parents who do not know, or do not understand, the programs and services that schools provide may not be as involved as parents who are informed and engaged.

School districts around the nation are trying hard to address this disparity, and have been doing so for many years (as with school busing). In most schools here in Metro Denver, which includes half a dozen or more different school districts, you will find a "parent liaison" who is tasked with engaging the parents and keeping them up to date with what is happening.

However, when cultural differences combine with a language barrier, the problem can be amplified.

Parents who do not speak English at home (parents who did not learn English as a child and currently speak a non-English language in the home) are less likely than other parents to attend a general school meeting or school event, or to volunteer or serve on a committee, or the PTA.

Parents who do not speak English well may feel less comfortable or less welcome getting involved in their children's schools.

Fluent communication between parents and teachers can lead to increased academic performance, positive social outcomes for children, and permanence in schools, as well as enable teachers to identify learning problems at an earlier age.

When teachers lack understanding of the cultural context of children and families, it can hinder children's development.

"When schools, families, and community groups work together to support learning, children tend to do better in school, stay in school longer, and like school more," according to the Southwest Educational Development Laboratory.

According to the organization, students with involved parents are more likely to:

- Earn higher grades and test scores, and enroll in higher-level programs

- Be promoted, pass their classes, and earn credits

- Attend school regularly

- Have better social skills, show improved behavior, and adapt well to school

- Graduate and go on to postsecondary education (Henderson & Mapp, 2002).

- Improve family income

Working to include parents is particularly important as students grow older and attend schools with high concentrations of poor and minority students (Rutherford et al., 1997).

Some suggestions for fostering parent/family engagement are:

- Help families with parenting and child-rearing skills

- Communicate with families about school programs and student progress and needs

- Work to improve recruitment, training, and schedules to involve families as volunteers in school activities

- Encourage families to be involved in learning activities at home

- Include parents as participants in important school decisions

- Coordinate with businesses and agencies to provide resources and services for families, students, and the community (Epstein, 2001)

Some parent liaisons are bilingual, and they are doing their best. But even bilingual isn't enough: Denver Public Schools support 83 distinct languages.

Many schools and parent liaisons create welcome events for the parents to come and get to know the school and each other. Potluck dinners are common.

But what happens at a casual gathering like this?

At most of these events, the English speakers go to one side of the gym, and the Spanish speakers go to the other.

Now consider the ShareLingo model, where it can be a "potluck with a purpose"—the purpose being to bring English and Spanish speakers together to practice.

When we bring a group of Spanish-speaking parents into the school to practice with a group of English-speaking teachers, administrators, and other parents, it forms a bond. The conversation topics and language vocabulary focus on the things important to everyone in the room: how to help kids who are struggling, the importance of reading at home, the programs and services available to families, and school safety issues.

ShareLingo support materials are tailored to meet the school and parent needs. Almost any of your school's bilingual materials can be incorporated. The important thing is to follow the ShareLingo model: capitalize on each participant's innate desire to understand and to be understood.

This kind of multicultural meeting represents parental engagement at its highest level. The parents are physically coming into the school and engaging, through language learning, with the people they are most afraid of—the teachers and administrators. As the fear and misunderstanding are eliminated, confidence and trust are built. Participants on BOTH sides open up and begin to understand the other's culture.

For you see, the misunderstandings and fears are not limited to just the immigrants!

In the Montbello neighborhood in North Denver, some schools are over 95 percent Hispanic. The teaching staff, meanwhile, is over 80 percent White. It's not that the district only hires Whites! The district is trying desperately to hire more diversity—sometimes even marketing to Puerto Rico and other Latin American countries for teachers!

We have another huge problem in our country. We don't pay our teachers nearly enough. It is a sad reality that it is very difficult to support a family on a teacher's salary. So this means that many teachers are young, enthusiastic kids, really. Many are fresh out of college. They're wonderful people who want to make a difference in the world. But many have not been exposed to the realities of the communities they may be teaching in.

Where I'm leading to is the fact that it is not just the immigrants who need to learn about our culture. We need to learn about and understand their culture and realities as well.

It's easy for a teacher to think, "Why don't these parents make their kids do their homework?" Well, perhaps the parents themselves aren't able to help. It could be because of a lack of education on their part. Or it could be that they are working two or three jobs just to make ends meet. And perhaps there isn't a nice quiet study place for the kids to do their homework. If lots of people are all living in a one- or two-bedroom apartment, it can be difficult to get quiet time. And it can be difficult to set aside time to do the homework.

When we can bring the parents into the school and start real, trusting conversations, these kinds of topics can be raised without fear or judgment. The friendly, collaborative nature of the ShareLingo program leads to real insights in both directions. Parents find out it's ok to ask questions (something they may NEVER do in their own countries), and educators can find out more about how they can help the parents and families help their kids.

## 6.5 LAW ENFORCEMENT

Culture can mean many things; it's not limited to race and ethnicity. Today, I think it's safe to say that tension between police and many citizens is a clash of cultures.

The overwhelming number of police, sheriffs, and immigration enforcement personnel that I've met have been extremely interested in improving community relations. I have even been to the ICE detention center in Aurora, and the people I met DO care about the people who are being detained. But they know that they are not trusted by the Spanish-speaking community.

**Is there any hope for bridging the gap between police and citizens—especially immigrants?**

### Scott and Carmen

A gentleman named Scott (name changed) wanted to learn Spanish. You see, his son was going to marry a woman who spoke Spanish. She was Cuban, from Miami. Scott, being the father of the groom, wanted to be able to give part of his speech at the wedding in Spanish. He heard about The ShareLingo Project and decided to join one of our groups. He did this on his own time and with his own money.

Carmen is an immigrant woman who has lived here for several years, and she wanted to improve her English. She wanted to do this so that she could understand her children's teachers, talk to the doctor, to perhaps get a better job, and to understand what was happening in the community around her. Carmen heard about the ShareLingo Project through a nonprofit that we had told about the program. Carmen joined the class and, although she received a discount through the nonprofit, paid for the class out of her own pocket.

On the first day of class, five English speakers and five Spanish speakers came together in a little house south of downtown, where we had our office at the time. We had a bilingual facilitator leading the group, and I was there also.

Scott and Carmen met each other for the first time in that group.

**Scott was a commander in the Police Department.**

He came to the class right after work in his crisp blue uniform.

With his big gold Commander badge.

And his handcuffs.

**And his gun.**

He took a seat at the big dining room table that we gathered around for that class.

Next to Carmen.

Now Carmen didn't volunteer anything about her immigration status, and this narrative is not intended to debate, or even comment on, documented vs. undocumented immigration.

But like many immigrants (and many non-immigrants as well), Carmen had a fear of authority in general and police specifically. Remember that:

**In some countries, the police may be the people you can least afford to trust.**

We started the class with introductions, like we always do, and I could see she was nervous. But she wasn't just nervous—she was scared. After we handed out materials and began to do the class,

**Carmen's hands were visibly shaking holding the first sheet of paper.**

But within just a couple of moments, Carmen settled down.

You see, what she [and the rest of the class] found out almost right away, was that Scott was not there for her, but to learn Spanish. Carmen was his partner that day, his teacher, and Scott was treating her with great respect.

He was grateful for her help. And he was also helping her learn English. He was nice to her. He was patient. He was HER teacher.

I saw Carmen sit up straighter in her chair. She smiled. I could see her relax. They even laughed together when one of them would mangle some pronunciation. It wasn't just that Scott was being nice—he acknowledged her intelligence and her expertise in a subject he was interested in.

Are you getting the significance of this? In just minutes, the atmosphere changed from deep DIS-trust, to confidence, then trust, then friendship.

Over the course of the 10 weekly sessions, Carmen and the entire class, including the other English speakers, became friends with Scott. The entire group was able to communicate with Scott AS friends. They could ask him tough questions—and he gave them honest answers.

Like, if you are a victim of a crime, you can call the police without fear—regardless of your residency status. Police here don't check papers. They help people. We all learned, for example, that if you're a mom suffering abuse and the police come to your door to help you, they're not going to take away your kids or send you back to your country, like your abuser may be telling you. Now, if you are the aggressor and the police arrest you, that's a very different matter, because SOMEONE is going to check your status, and you may have something to worry about.

Back to my story.

During the 10 weeks, the class helped Scott draft, translate, and practice his father-of-the-groom speech. I got to see it. It wasn't long, but it was significant, and it was from the heart.

Scott related what happened at the wedding to me while I was in his office one day talking about how we might be able to roll out ShareLingo for the Denver Police Department. As he was on the airplane traveling to Miami, he was practicing the Spanish in his head. Although he had practiced with the group, he was naturally nervous. He had not told anyone in the bride's family, or even his own family, that he was doing this.

So, after the wedding, they were all sitting at the long table of honor at the front of the wedding reception, eating and talking. Eventually, the toasts and speeches started. And then it was his turn. When he got up to talk, he began in English as normal. But about halfway through, he switched to Spanish. His son and the whole audience were surprised.

In my mind, I can see those surprised faces. I can hear the murmur of the crowd.

[I'm White too. And this happens to me sometimes (on a much smaller scale) when I speak Spanish to a person or group that doesn't expect it.]

It was not a long speech, but he finished it by turning to the bride and saying

**"Bienvenida a nuestra familia."**
**[Welcome to our family.]**

And the little Cuban girl, in her high heels and red lipstick, with tears in her eyes, rushed over to him, and gave him a HUGE hug and a kiss that left its mark on his cheek. He said he couldn't have been happier.

To be clear, this was a Cuban family in Miami, not some people fresh off the boat from El Salvador. They all spoke English. Scott did not have to make that gesture, but he did. Because Scott is that kind of guy. The father of the bride came to Scott, shook his hand, gave him the Latino "man-hug" and offered his thanks and gratitude for such a gesture.

That meaningful gesture strengthened the bond between the two families. It demonstrated and embraced the acceptance of the cultural differences.

And I think it illustrates the power and effectiveness of what ShareLingo is all about.

Is Scott unique? By that I mean, is Scott the only officer here who wants to learn Spanish? Nope—I talk to police all the time. I ask, "Do you speak Spanish?"

And as with the general community, the overwhelming response is, "I Wish."

If we can get more police practicing language with more of the community, nothing but good can come of it.

If you work in law enforcement, please consider implementing a ShareLingo-style group that can help English-speaking police connect with the Hispanic community that you serve and protect. You won't just learn Spanish—you will also better understand the culture and the community. And you will build trust.

# 6.6 FAITH-BASED COMMUNITIES

## Churches

Ever since the first days of ShareLingo, I have believed that churches and the faith-based community would benefit greatly by helping English and Spanish speakers connect. As you may notice in the "About the Author" section of this book, I was helping with ESL classes at Centro San Juan Diego, the Catholic Archdiocese Hispanic Outreach Center, when I had the idea to start a ShareLingo-style program. Of course, at that time, I didn't know how far it would lead—I just thought there should be a place where English and Spanish speakers could teach each other and practice together.

Many churches are self-segregated because they do not offer services in both English and Spanish. So, it is common to see two churches side-by-side—one fully in English and the other fully in Spanish.

But not all churches, by any means, are limited to just one language.

I go to a different church here in Aurora, Colorado. The congregation is made up of roughly 65% Hispanic members. Services are offered in both English and Spanish every weekend. One priest is from Spain, another from Colombia. and the third, who is from Cameroon, speaks Bassa, English, French, and Italian, and is learning Spanish. Keep in mind that Aurora represents people who speak something like 140 different languages. Our church does not have services in French, Vietnamese, or Russian—at least not yet—so the English services are more ethnically mixed than the Spanish services.

Each week, in the same building, I see the English-speaking community come to the church for worship. As they are leaving, the Spanish-speaking community comes for their services. (I happen to prefer the Spanish services—they are much more vibrant, full of family and celebration on a scale that is not matched at the English services.)

It's a pretty large church, with an expansive main worship area, classrooms, and even a gym. There is something going on there every day, and it is quite common for one presentation or another to be in English while something else is taking place in Spanish elsewhere in the building.

Partly with the help of ShareLingo, the church is taking steps to unite the two communities. Not only are many people learning English at the church, but many are learning Spanish as well. There are dinners, weddings, funerals, and other events where the two communities cross over, at least to some extent. But it could be better. It's getting better. Of course, whenever possible, the church leaders TRY to include both communities. There just aren't that many programs that can accomplish this goal.

My church is not unique. This "two-communities-sharing-one-space" is common throughout the U.S. today. I hope that more and more churches adopt a ShareLingo-style model for helping their communities connect.

If your church is serving both the English- and Spanish-speaking communities, a ShareLingo-style program can help you enormously. You can begin to bring the two communities together in a way that no other type of program does.

## Missions

Americans, and church communities in particular, are just so generous in so many ways. Many churches sponsor mission trips to help other communities in one way or another. It may be through building shelter, feeding and clothing the poor, or improving health, education, or any number of services. Sometimes, the mission work is within the same city, where a more fortunate community may help out one that is less fortunate. But often, mission trips involve travel to another country. And certainly, due to our proximity to Central and South America, many destinations involve Spanish speakers.

I know many people who have participated in mission trips. In almost every instance, the experience was life changing—rewarding beyond belief.

But here's the thing—sometimes I question whether we are giving the people in other countries (or communities) what they really need, or what we think they need, because it may not be the same thing. When we go to another country, I think it is important that we don't fall into the trap of thinking what may be good for Americans is necessarily good for the people of that country. For example, suppose we decide to go someplace and "build a school." That sounds great, right? Because education is possibly the single best way to help someone escape poverty. But if we simply go and build a school building, and don't provide the resources to run that school, or don't provide a path for success for the kids that go to that school, then what good is it? And how do we KNOW what is good for a community if we don't ASK? And how can we ask, if we don't understand the culture, and the LANGUAGE?

For this reason, I think it's important that every mission volunteer learn as much as they can about the language and culture of their target destination before they set off. I think it is important for the mission participants to ask the people they want to help what they really need. And then, as much as possible, I think we need to give the local people the resources (money and talent) to do what needs to be done themselves. *Teach a man to fish...*

Mission trips come in two main flavors: The short, couple-of-week version, and the longer, year-or-more version. I certainly believe that it helps every person going on a mission trip to know at least "enough" of the language of the people they are going to serve. I've found that the vast majority of the people I meet who are going on the shorter trips don't prep in advance—but of the ones I've spoken with about this, they all, without exception, have told me that they wish they had.

Many of the people I know who have done the longer trips did have an opportunity to study the language prior to departing. But rarely, if ever, the culture. And they all told me that they didn't REALLY learn the language until they got there and were FORCED to use it. They have told me that the first few days or weeks were really stressful. Even though they had learned some words and phrases, they hadn't really PRACTICED, so they weren't prepared for that level of immersion. ShareLingo-style sessions can help lessen the blow. And speaking with native speakers prior to the trip can help with another aspect as well—the culture shock.

If I were to decide to go to Nicaragua or El Salvador on a mission trip of this kind, I would make an effort to find some people here in Denver who are from Nicaragua or El Salvador. I would be interested in learning their language and getting accustomed to their accents. I would also love to ask them about any cultural differences. Common greetings and customs would be a start, so I don't make some unintentional mistake. And it would be an opportunity to better understand what their countries might need, long before I even go there.

Moving to another country for a year isn't just stressful because of the language. We cannot forget, or underestimate, the cultural impacts. "Culture Shock" can be extreme. And this is another important benefit of meeting and practicing with someone from that country in advance.

## Derek's Story:

Derek Bearman is actually the person helping me formally proofread this manuscript. It seems my punctuation is pretty bad! But Derek also speaks Spanish because of his mission work in Argentina some years ago. So I asked Derek to comment on his experience:

James is 100% correct when he says that mission trips (especially those of a year or longer) are life-changing. I was in Argentina from May of 2012 until May of 2014. Well, let me backtrack a bit—the organization that sponsored my mission is The Church of Jesus Christ of Latter-day Saints, and part of their program includes going to a place in Provo, Utah called the Missionary Training Center. All missionaries who are sent around the world first go through the Missionary Training Center to be brought up to speed on the purpose of their mission. The nature of the mission of every missionary who goes through the MTC is religious, so we would learn how to teach others our religion (even for English speakers, this required a bit of "translation," to say the least). When I was at the MTC, though, not only were my studies focused on the doctrines and principles of our religion, but also on learning the language of the people I was called to serve. I spent a total of two months in the MTC learning the basics of Spanish before I even set out for Argentina.

Once my training at the MTC was finally complete (you can only learn so much without some degree of immersion), it was time for me to fly to the other side of the world and put my Spanish skills to the test. However, due to a delay with the approval of my visa application, I ended up going to Wisconsin for a few months while I waited. I didn't make it to Argentina until October of 2012 even though my mission had already begun. The reason I mention this delay at all is because it gave me a couple different tastes of the Spanish language and Hispanic culture before my total immersion in Argentina.

While in the MTC, we were taught by other gringos who had gone through the same process of learning Spanish through their own immersive mission experiences. They knew Spanish very well, and they taught very well, but what we were learning was basically second-hand knowledge and experience. Learning from a gringo who speaks Spanish as a second language is different than learning through conversation with a native Spanish speaker. While I was in Wisconsin awaiting my visa to be approved, yes, I was still in the States, but we primarily worked with Mexican families who spoke little-to-no English, and the English they did know was fairly broken. This was my first "real" experience with practicing my Spanish with native speakers. As confident as I thought I was after my two-month training at the MTC, I soon realized that my Spanish was far more broken than was the English spoken by those we served. My competency in speaking Spanish with the Mexican-American families improved a bit, but boy was I in for a rude awakening in Argentina.

As soon as I stepped off the plane in Buenos Aires, I was on an alien planet. Think for a moment about your own confidence and comfort with our American culture when you're out and about running errands, going shopping, or just hanging out at the mall. Most of the time, you will encounter a substantial amount of other people out in public, right? If you were to ever want to, you could easily eavesdrop on any conversation within your vicinity, and even the conversations that are just out of earshot you can usually at least determine are spoken in English. If there are not many people around, you will still often find some kind of noise that is in English, whether it be something on TV, a song, or a commercial. As you look up and around at street signs, banners, storefronts, or advertisements, 99% of what you see is written in English. Even if there are all of these things occurring at once and you can hardly focus on any one of them at a time, you can at least be comfortable in understanding what you see and hear. English is in the air; it is in the atmosphere; it is the ambient noise in your life almost anywhere you find yourself.

Now imagine that all of that—the street signs, the conversations, the songs, the advertisements, the businesses—is in *Spanish*. Imagine that no matter how hard you focus on any visual or auditory stimulus, you *cannot* understand a single word of it. You don't even know where to begin to look for a shred of familiarity or direction. Spanish is in the air. The entire world around you is in Spanish.

***That*** is how I felt when I stepped off of the plane in Buenos Aires, Argentina. I was smack-dab in the middle of an alien world.

Talk about culture shock, huh? Ha! That's not even the half of it.

I could spend hours, even days, writing about my experience in Argentina. I was there for over a year and a half, every day learning ever more about the culture and language of the people there. As I stated before, I was on a mission for my church, and the nature of that mission was very religious. However, even though seeking out those willing to hear our message and inviting them to commit to be baptized into the church was the official expressed goal of our work, we were repeatedly reminded by our mission leaders, ourselves, and even our religious scripture study material that the highest mission of anyone ought to be to serve others. Ultimately, it didn't matter how many people we led to baptism; what mattered was how we spent our time in the service of others—in blessing their lives the best we could.

There are a variety of ways we as missionaries strove to serve the Argentine people, but the main one relevant to this project was that of teaching others English. *So many people* in Argentina want to know English. Our purpose at the time was not necessarily to teach English, but the interest in it was strong in every area we visited, so we did the best we could. My exposure to the Argentine culture and language were what forced me to push myself and increase my proficiency in Spanish. I came home from that experience fluent in the language and with a new fire and determination to learn as many languages as I can cram into one lifetime.

Anyway, this book isn't about me, but I can attest to the benefits of being bilingual. I have gained an appreciation and respect for people of foreign cultures; the pool of people I can now comfortably communicate with has expanded; I have a new skill under my belt that I can leverage in the workplace; and I have a somewhat forward-thinking perspective on life and all of us who live on this rock floating through space.

This relation of my story is far longer than I anticipated it to be (like I said, I could go on for hours), but the reason for that is learning a second language has opened my eyes in ways I didn't even know they were shut. No matter what the language or the culture you want to learn and understand, a program such as ShareLingo that provides a structured approach to such learning by mixing and mingling domestics and foreigners is by far the best way to do so. Not everyone will have the opportunity for full immersion—it's simply not realistic. Affiliating yourself and picking the brains of people from different cultures is literally the next best thing, though, and exponentially more attainable than is travelling halfway around the world. Whether you are skeptical about this approach or not, if you truly want to learn a second language and lift the world where you stand, take the leap. You won't be disappointed.

## 6.7 NONPROFITS

Nonprofits are very, very dear to my heart. I really struggled with the decision whether to form ShareLingo as a nonprofit, or as a Social Enterprise. As you'll see in the "How ShareLingo Started" section, I chose the social enterprise approach. But it was not for lack of appreciation for the ethics and impact of the nonprofit sector.

For information about Social Enterprise see this link: http://bit.ly/BWResource13

Do you work for, or with, a nonprofit? If so, chances are good that you are strapped for cash at a time when there is more and more need for your services. Chances are also good that you are experiencing a greater mix of Spanish-speaking people needing your services.

One area in particular where we see this happening is healthcare. Nonprofits are helping with prenatal care, dentistry, drug addiction, AIDS, obesity, and just about every other aspect of healthcare in America today.

In fact, nonprofits are being called upon more and more today to pick up the slack throughout our communities as governments cut back on services. Another area where we see the need is in education, where nonprofits are helping provide books and other materials, and even staff, in order to pick up the slack.

We all think of Goodwill as that place we take our unwanted clothes and furniture. But do you know what they do with the money they generate? Lots. For example, did you know that Goodwill Industries provides staff in many schools to help mentor kids?

For all the positive that nonprofits do, the world around them seems to be so negative.

Kevin, a good friend who's the executive director of a nonprofit here in Denver, posted: "Wow, still so much anger and seething over the election outcome. It seems we used to be able to talk about policy issues; now we are choosing sides in a new-age civil war. Are we too far gone to return to civility?"

I'm one of the people who think we have NOT gone too far. There are lots of reasons to still have hope and confidence that we CAN return to civility.

Nonprofits, in fact, are where civility is nurtured.

Jocelyn Miller is the executive director of the Robert A. Miller Educational Resource Center (RAMERC) in the Skyland/North City Park area of Denver.

Ever since she first founded the center after her father's death, Jocelyn has welcomed everyone through her doors, regardless of race, language, or economic status. Although the Skyland/North City Park area has been predominantly African American for many years, the neighborhood is changing. More and more white and Hispanic families are moving in.

Jocelyn applied for (and won) a grant from the city of Denver to hold ShareLingo classes in her center on an ongoing basis. This grant, along with an in-kind contribution on the part of ShareLingo, will allow both the English and Spanish speakers to attend the classes for free. (ShareLingo is working towards being able to offer classes to ALL nonprofits without charge—not there yet, but getting closer.)

I sat down with Jocelyn and learned that her mission to bring communities together in support of families has its roots in the examples set by her father:

> Robert A. Miller was an African American renaissance man—he spoke three languages and was

a musician, a world traveler, a community leader, and a psychiatric social worker.

He worked with Denver Health for a time, and would often go to Native American reservations to make sure the kids had shoes and coats. But all was not rosy. These were hard times for people of color in Colorado. Through it all, Mr. Miller taught Jocelyn, and the people around him, that when dealing with racism, they should not resort to using anger. People need to care about people—no matter what they look like.

For a while, he worked in Walsenburg, Colorado, (in southern Colorado, about four hours from Denver) where he was the only black man in the whole town. He spoke Spanish, and his neighbors knew and trusted him. But not everyone did.

He worked in Walsenburg during the week, and went back to Denver to be with his family on weekends. He told Jocelyn of one trip driving from Walsenburg to Denver. He got pulled over by two sheriff's cars—one ahead of him, and one behind. They made him pull off the highway and drive into an old barn. When he was inside that barn, he was terrified—he said these men could have done anything to him, and the sheriffs went off to "discuss" something. He said he just kept praying and praying. They kept talking.

Then finally one said, "get out of here boy," and he was allowed to drive away.

Can you even imagine? How can that not make a person angry? But it didn't. And even though this wasn't an isolated incident, Mr. Miller continued to be an example for us all—building kindness and friendship wherever he went.

One of the things Mr. Miller was passionate about was teaching the black community the importance of buying property. At one point, he had three rental properties in Denver, and the duplex where the Center (RAMERC) is now located was one of them.

Jocelyn tells me that when he bought the house in the '50s, the area was very multicultural, with Japanese, white, and black families all living nearby. By the '80s, it became predominantly African American, and by 2005, when Jocelyn founded RAMERC, the neighborhood started shifting to more Hispanic.

The RAMERC is a grassroots, nonprofit organization that provides education materials and support services for children, at-risk families, educators, and caregivers, with a focus on health—in the broadest meaning of the term.

Jocelyn says she adapts to the needs of the community—empowering women of color one day, helping Spanish speakers to learn English another, and teaching children to garden and eat healthfully yet another day. "Stuff just flows," she said, pointing to a "love comes in all colors" poster on the wall.

The father planted the seed of civility, and the daughter keeps it growing strong.

That's what I see when I work with the nonprofits in my world.

*A ShareLingo class at RAMERC—*
*Connecting Cultures through Language*

If you are working in a non profit, I applaud you. I thank you. And I want to help you if I can. Please reach out to me—whether it is simply for someone to listen, or to help you learn Spanish, or to help your organization connect the English- and Spanish-speaking communities.

## 6.8 SALES AND SERVICE

As I mentioned earlier, the Hispanic market in this country is fast approaching $1.5 trillion in value. If you are not reaching out to the Hispanic market, you're missing a HUGE, still mostly untapped, potential.

Did you know that the U.S. Hispanic market is bigger than the entire Canadian market? (*http://bit.ly/BWVideo5*)

Hispanics are one-fifth of the U.S. population and will continue to grow as one out of every two babies born in the U.S. is Hispanic.

So who is this Hispanic population?

Many are bilingual—some are not. But even if they are bilingual, many recall and like Spanish-speaking ads more than English-speaking ads. It's just a fact. And being bilingual is cool now. It's celebrated. Younger people are no longer ashamed (thank God) that they speak Spanish at home and English at school.

> I speak Spanish, but when I've visited places like Costa Rica or Colombia, I noticed and remembered ads in English much more than all those ads in Spanish, which just blended into the clutter.
>
> Have you ever been to a Mexican supermarket? If not, why not? I'm sure you see them all the time, right? They're AWESOME! You can get the best cheese there. You know, that stuff you LOVE on the enchiladas in your favorite Mexican restaurant?

Companies like Coke, Pepsi, Ford, and even REMAX have commercials in Spanish now. Here in Denver, Telemundo is now the No. 1 station for evening news.

People don't "press 2 for Spanish" because they demand it. They do it because the companies are marketing to and supporting them!

A few weeks ago, I was having a lot of trouble with my website. I had to call for support lots of times. Normally, I go to the English support, right? I'm more comfortable talking about tech stuff in English. But one time I was told, by the automated attendant, that the hold time for support was over an hour. Now, every time I called, I would always hear that message—"Para español, marque dos," but I always ignored it. This time, I hung up, and dialed back. I pressed 2 for Spanish. On that occasion, the hold time to reach someone who spoke Spanish was TWO MINUTES. Seriously. One hour for English, two minutes for Spanish. And, as I was talking to them in Spanish and describing my problem, I asked where they were located. I was thinking Costa Rica, Colombia, or another South American country where multinationals have tech support teams standing by. It turned out the support person was in Arizona. She spoke perfect English too!

## Retail

Lowe's and Home Depot have had bilingual signs and materials for several years now. And they've come a long way. I remember a few years ago when Lowe's first started switching over to include materials in Spanish. I was with a native Spanish speaker and we looked at a flyer for something that was in Spanish—I think it was a washing machine—and she laughed. She said, "This flyer is marketing to Gringos in Spanish!" Lowe's had had the English flyer translated to Spanish, without taking into account the cultural differences. Latinos don't buy washing machines for the same reasons we do. Well, sure, they want to wash clothes. But what motivates them to purchase a particular brand or feature is different.

So my friend was right. By simply translating the flyer, they were marketing to someone like me, an American; but in Spanish. It was a pretty useless flyer. I still commend them for seeing the writing on the wall and taking the initiative to address the Hispanic market way back then, and they are doing way better now.

If you really want a great example of how a store markets to their customers in different languages, go to Walmart. I have to hand it to them—they do make it a point to know what their customers want. When they translate something, not only the language is considered, but every nuance of the culture as well.

One more retail example:

I have Comcast cable here for TV, Phone, and Internet. And now, Comcast has "retail" outlets. These are actual stores you can go to to pay your bill, get new service, pick up or drop off equipment, etc. I'm noticing now that way more clients are Spanish speakers, and way more of the attendants are bilingual.

But since I'm speaking about Comcast, let's look at service, specifically the installation.

I was having new cable service installed in my home. Not surprisingly, the guy who came to do the installation spoke English. But I am me, so I asked, "Do you speak Spanish?" (Because of ShareLingo, I ask pretty much everybody that.) The answer was: "I wish."

As the conversation went on, the installer told me that he has had many occasions where he had gone to do an install and the person there spoke only Spanish. Maybe Abuela [Grandma] is left behind while the other people go to work, and she doesn't speak English. So then there was a lot of pointing and gesturing and trying to explain why he couldn't put the cable in one place, and it had to go to another place—like, he couldn't run a cable through a doorway, for example. NO BUENO. NO BUENO.

So how do all these examples lead back to creating bilingual, cross-cultural, language groups?

If you have a Ford dealership, and you want to bring in more Hispanic customers, how about instead of another ad that says, "We have the best cars and lowest prices," you say, "Come in for a test drive and practice English with our staff." (In Spanish, of course.) You can help the immigrant community learn more English and bring people into your dealership at the same time. And you know what else? You will learn the particular tastes of your potential Hispanic consumer. What colors do they like? What tires do they like? What are their buying habits? In a ShareLingo-style group, you can get lots of answers you just can't get from random visitors, or even a focus group.

And if your business relies on installers or other service providers, don't you think it might be a good idea to have them know at least enough Spanish to do a great install?

## 6.9 LOVE AND FAMILY (AND DATING)— WAIT. WHAT??

Obviously, dating is not an economic "sector."

And ShareLingo is by no means a "dating" program.

But romance often happens when people meet people.

People want to meet people who are different from themselves.

One of the most powerful motivators for learning a language is to meet someone "foreign" who speaks another language.

Why is this? Why do so many of us find someone from another country *exotic*?

While humanity often has a "tribal" mentality—that is, we join with the members of our tribe to protect ourselves from outsiders—there is one enormous exception. When it comes to finding a mate, we are also instinctively drawn to people who are different from us.

Consider the opposite: "inbreeding." We all know that it weakens the gene pool. That's why it's gross to date your sister (or brother) no matter how good looking they may be to other people. Most people also know that diversity, on the other hand, strengthens the gene pool. Marrying outside your clan makes the clan stronger.

In today's society, with so many people migrating to different cities and states (and countries), it is much easier to meet someone from "outside your village." And there are more and more "mixed" marriages—the offspring of which are often recognized as especially beautiful children. Am I right?!

But this desire for, this fascination with, this ATTRACTION TO, people who are not from our own community is powerful, having been developed over millions of years.

How do we find those people?

Sure, it's easy to see that someone from a different race is "outside your clan." People who look different from us, our family, and our neighbors are intriguing. Personally, I'm pretty stoked that interracial marriages are much more common these days.

But sometimes, many times, people outside our own community simply SPEAK differently than we do. People from Iowa look pretty much the same as people from Boston or Texas or much of Europe. But they don't SOUND the same!

We find their accents "exotic" also.

*"OH! I just love the way she speaks."*

Accent. Dialect. The way they speak.

Aside from race, facial features, and skin color, having a different accent is the next-most obvious distinguishing factor. And it's powerful.

Think of Sofia Vargera, Sean Connery, and so many other examples from TV and movies.

Yes, they are attractive looking. But it's not just their looks that attract us. Those accents draw us in.

In our classes at ShareLingo, we are careful to make this distinction between pronunciation and accent.

So many people come to us and are self-conscious, maybe even embarrassed, about their accent. So we reinforce that their ACCENT is beautiful. We actually encourage them NOT to lose their accent. But they do have to be very focused on pronunciation—and clarity. There's a big difference between "boss" and "bus," and the pronunciation nuance is tricky for Spanish speakers.

This takes tons of practice.

Because of what I do, I meet a lot of people from "mixed marriages." The vast majority are American guys who have met and married Latinas. Yet, the women are taking our ShareLingo courses in order to improve their English. Why is that? After all, they live with a native English speaker. But they don't feel that their English is improving. And, to a large extent, they are right.

There are three reasons for this.

1. Their partner has learned how to understand them. Whether it is an accent, Spanglish, or even hand signals,—the two communicate. They know

each other's habits, styles, and desires. So, the partner just "gets it" and has stopped correcting their spouse. Here's an example. I have a friend who says "Remember me" when she really means "Remind Me" (of something she's forgotten.) It's a habit, but I know what she means, and I don't normally correct her any more – I just know what she means.

2. It's hard to learn anything from your spouse (or kids). If you have ever tried to teach your partner to do something—ski, play tennis, play chess, paint, etc.—you may know what I'm talking about. Far better to invest in a coach (a stranger) to help them. Saves a lot of arguments.

3. Cuteness—seriously. So many guys (in the couples I see most) tell me, "Oh, I just love her accent. I don't want it to change. Even when she's mad at me, her accent is just beautiful!" These guys don't WANT their partners to lose their accents! I try to reassure them that helping with pronunciation is not going to take away their accent. Their partner will still be just as CUTE!

A special note about kids and cultures:

Many, many of our immigrant participants—mostly women, but men too—join our classes because they want to better understand what their kids are saying. Immigrant kids are learning English in school. Not just in the classroom, but also by just playing with their friends. They lose their accents, and become native speakers in two languages. They have to, and they do. It becomes easy for them (eventually). And then even at home, although they may speak to their parents in Spanish, siblings talk to each other in English.

So the next logical question is, if the kids are fluent in English, why don't they teach their parents English? Believe it or not, it's even harder than teaching your spouse. One problem is, it's just hard to teach your parents. The whole dynamic is different. It has to do with patience, respect, and just a whole lot of issues.

But the bigger problem, in most cases, is being self-conscious. In many cultures, and maybe especially so in Latino cultures, it's really common to make fun of other people, and that is doubly so for your family. If someone trips or stubs their toe, you laugh. If someone struggles, you laugh. Maybe it's a mechanism for dealing with disappointment and hardship. But I do know that these parents have been laughed at—over and over—by their own children. Say a kid is 8 years old and speaks English really well. The parent tries to say "sheet of paper." The kid laughs and laughs! "You said 'Shit' mom! HA HA HA HA HA."

Maybe the parent laughs too. But inside, they hurt. So the parent stops trying. They stop speaking English in front of their kids—or anybody.

**Does learning a language help you find a date?**

ABSOLUTELY.

Whether you are going to another country or you've met someone here, being able to open the door to communication changes everything.

There are blogs dedicated to this one aspect of why to learn a language—dating. For example: *http://bit.ly/BWResource8*

> In this blog, James Maverick tells a great story and makes a great observation. He met a girl from Cali, Colombia, in Copenhagen, Denmark. The conversation started in English, the common language there. The girl was being aloof, reserved. But since she looked Latina, he asked where she was from. Upon learning that she was from Colombia, he switched to Spanish. Her eyes lit up with surprise, and he says, "From that point on, I began conversing with a completely different person. I witnessed her icy personality melt before my very eyes. What was initially a very aloof and distant person suddenly transformed into a warm, sexy, and flirtatious girl. She loosened up. She smiled."

The point I want to highlight in Maverick's story is this: People think and act differently in different languages. In English, this girl was aloof and distant, like the people tended to be in that culture. But when they switched to Spanish, she became "herself," and, as Maverick put it, she "returned to her wonderful roots."

Even if you are in the United States, and even if the person you are interested in speaks English, speaking some of THEIR language will really help set you apart. More than that, the process of learning the other person's language will introduce you to their culture. So maybe you won't make a terrible, culturally sensitive mistake!

Finally, even if you aren't so much interested in dating—perhaps you are very happily married to your high school sweetheart and you simply aren't looking to find a Spanish-speaking life partner—the chances are that you KNOW someone who has a mixed (English/Spanish) marriage. Wouldn't it be amazing to <u>really</u> get to know them?!

This is your chance!

## 6.10 GOVERNMENT

At the federal, state, and local levels, government is changing. And, while I see lots of tension at the national level, I see lots to be encouraged about at the state and local levels.

With the past President, Obama, we saw the pendulum shift one direction. And with the current President, Trump, we have seen it shift very much in the opposite direction.

At the state level, more and more minority representatives are becoming governors and state legislators. The people are speaking.

This shift certainly includes Hispanics. Crisanta Duran, a wonderful person, just became the first Latina Speaker of the House here in Colorado. Not surprisingly, she has a lot of support from the Hispanic community—and she cares deeply about Latino issues. But to become Speaker, you have to have the support of a much broader community. You have to be recognized by your party, and so, your constituents, as someone who can get things done. So you have to have the support of both sides of the house. You have to be someone who can build bridges. Crisanta is that kind of person.

If you are working at the federal or state level, you can make a huge impact to reduce fear and distrust in so many areas! Please contact me!

But for now, I would like to focus on the local level, because that is where I see so much hope for so many communities. After all, it is at the local level where we spend the most important parts of our lives: where we find food and shelter; where we build friendships and community; and where we find day care, education, and support services.

Cities are developing programs to build bridges between citizens who speak different languages: Mountain View, California, provides information about all of its services in four different languages; Memphis, Tennessee, sends its police and fire officials across the city to talk about safety in multiple languages; in Lewiston, Maine, stories from new immigrants are collected and translated and published in a book to preserve heritage and build community awareness. Libraries have also become a place where learning happens in many languages. So many great programs are underway: you can find descriptions in this report from the National League of Cities: *http://bit.ly/BWResource12*


When we dig down to individual neighborhoods and help one neighbor talk to another, we can start a movement! I believe that movement will bubble UP to the state and national levels.

At the local level, it is now common for elected officials—mayors, councilmen/women—to be very much a part of the community they represent. If an area is primarily Hispanic or Asian or African American, it's much more likely than in the past that their representatives reflect that community. And no matter what your race or background may be, you better believe that if you want to get reelected, you have to be listening to ALL of your constituents.

In my community here—Metro Denver in general, and Aurora specifically—I am seeing this. Like many urban areas, Metro Denver is actually made up of several connected cities, and thus, several government entities. In addition to the City and County of Denver, we have Lakewood, Golden, Arvada, Aurora, Centennial, etc. Each one has its own mayor, its own city council, and its own local laws. There are many individual school districts, police forces, and fire departments.

Chances are, if you are reading this section, you work in local government in some way. Maybe you're a mayor, or maybe you are a lifeguard at the local swimming pool. Either way, you can make a difference.

Of course, different parts of the community have different levels of immigrant densities and "pockets" of one ethnicity or another. These are not just Hispanic. There are people from all parts of Russia, Asia, Africa, and Europe. Of course, there are also people from Central and South America.

Since I live in Aurora, I'd like to highlight what I'm seeing here, because I believe it is a great example.

Aurora, Colorado, is located on the east side of Denver and is home to a very diverse population.

In the '90s, finding a bilingual person (of any language) was very rare in the Aurora city government. Today, that has changed a LOT.

In fact, Aurora has produced a Comprehensive Strategic Plan within their Office of International and Immigrant Affairs. That document quotes several statements from the National League of Cities and the Migration Policy Institute. (*http://bit.ly/BWResource9*)

In the Comprehensive Plan, Steve Hogan, Aurora's mayor, states: "People from about 140 countries make their home in this community because they feel welcome, find opportunity, and achieve success." And he continues, "True integration happens at the local level, and cities and local officials play a key role in that integration process."

Within the plan, there are eight distinct goals to be undertaken by the city related to successful integration. (I've emphasized the text that relates to statements that I have made within this book.)

## A. INTEGRATION THROUGH CIVIC ENGAGEMENT

- **"Engaging immigrants and refugees in the civic life of the city, by promoting naturalization among newcomers, will help local governments foster a more welcoming environment and encourage greater civic participation among our new residents."** (National League of Cities)

## B. SAFETY IN OUR INTERNATIONAL CITY

- **"Police-immigrant relationships are essential for effective community policing, and public safety outreach is crucial for immigrants and refugees accustomed to different cultures and police expectations."** (National League of Cities)

## C. INTEGRATING THROUGH LANGUAGE ACQUISITION

- **Produce a new television series to teach ESL and civics through the public library** system, community partners, and Communications/Aurora TV. This television series will include tutorials, live discussions between teachers and students, and information on civics and American culture.

- Support expansion of ESL classes and adult education programs throughout the city.

- Create public and private partnerships to create more accessible ESL opportunities.

- Promote English-language instruction information and community resources for English-language learners in the Aurora Public Library system.

- Extend opportunities to learn a second language for Aurorans wanting to communicate with newcomers for business and social purposes.

## D. INTEGRATION IN THE NEIGHBORHOODS

- "Immigrants and refugees face a unique set of challenges in accessing city services due to the **language barrier, lack of trust in government, and cultural differences.**" (National League of Cities)

## E. INTEGRATING THROUGH ECONOMIC AND FINANCIAL GROWTH

- "While **immigrants tend to set up businesses at higher rates than their native-born peers**, they face greater obstacles such as limited access to capital and financial services, a lack of familiarity with the local markets and business environment, and lack of knowledge about resources and programs for entrepreneurs." (Migration Policy Institute)

## F. INTERNATIONALITY AS A DRIVING FORCE FOR ECONOMIC DEVELOPMENT

- In order to continue to grow and become a key player at the international level, international strategic partnerships and collaborations in the areas of economics, culture, medicine, and business must be developed.

## G. INTEGRATING THROUGH SPORTS AND RECREATION

## H. INTEGRATING THROUGH ARTS AND CULTURE

ALL of these initiatives are important and commendable.

But, naturally, I would like to focus on section C, which relates specifically to language learning.

In section C, the City of Aurora has identified the importance of language learning for integrating the communities. Seems obvious, right? But what I want to highlight is that Aurora is not only thinking about teaching immigrants English. Aurora has set a goal to **"Extend opportunities to learn a second language for Aurorans wanting to communicate with newcomers for business and social purposes."** This isn't by accident. Aurora did a lot of work and research to come up with this plan.

This is so forward thinking! I am proud to live in a city where it is recognized that language is NOT a one-way street. It's **important** to make city government and its services accessible by translating information into its citizens' languages. It's **transformational** to go the next step and help residents grow and broaden their language and cultural skills.

# 7.0 How to Learn a Language

*"If you want to learn something, read about it.
If you want to understand something, write about
it. If you want to master something, teach it."*
**–Yogi Bhajan**

**Perhaps you want to learn Spanish for yourself.
Or perhaps you want to help English and Spanish
speakers in your school, hospital, factory, or
jobsite connect and learn from each other.**

This chapter describes what you need to know.

### Foundation *and* Practice

To learn a new language, here's what you need: foundation and practice. It's just like anything—playing the piano, for example. You need to know the basics in order to get started, and then you need to practice.

That's simple, right? (I'm an Engineer. I like to break things down and simplify them.)

Each of these two things has two parts:

| Foundation | Practice |
|---|---|
| 1.  Vocabulary | 1.  Listening |
| 2.  Grammar | 2.  Speaking |

The good news is you can do almost all of this by yourself—on your own.

Everything except the speaking part. Keep reading.

First, the **foundation.**

**Vocabulary:**

You can't tell someone to run unless you know the word for run (*correr* in Spanish). You can't say you have a dog unless you know the word for dog (perro). You can't say, "Have a nice day," if you don't know the word for day (Día). You will need to gradually learn new vocabulary. That's a process.

Some people tell me they just can't learn Spanish. They've tried, but they just can't. They think that they are too old, or that their brain won't accept another language.

That's garbage.

Suppose you know nothing about fly fishing (I don't either, actually) but you want to learn how to fly fish because it's out in nature, it's active, and you have a friend who loves fly fishing.

So you take up fly fishing—what happens? Next thing you know, you're out there, learning from your friend. They teach you some new words! Next time you're at a sporting goods store, you check out the fly fishing section and see all kinds of things that are new to you. You learn a few more new words for some new equipment.

You get online and find fly fishing websites. And you learn some more new words—like "wooly buggers, nymphs, and little black stoneflies." (I just learned these myself—check out the Orvis.com web site.)

My POINT is—you just learned some new words. In English.

You learned new words.

Well—if you can learn a new word in English, you can learn one in Spanish, or any other language. It's the same part of the brain.

Let me say that again—**The same part of your brain that logs English does any other language as well. So yes, you CAN learn a new language.**

El vaso = The glass

Está = is (to be)

Encima de= on top of (above)

La mesa = The table

The glass is on the table = El vaso está encima de la mesa.

Now every time you think about a glass, think of it as a "vaso." Use Spanglish: *"Pass me the vaso. I'll have a vaso of water."*

Next thing you know, you KNOW. Vaso is glass. When you say vaso, you can picture a glass in your head—just like you do now with "glass."

The process is WAY easier than you think it is.

Pronunciation is a different matter—that's muscular, like hitting a baseball. That takes more practice. I'll talk about practice in a minute.

**Grammar:**

How do you distinguish between *I run* and *I ran*? (*Corro* vs *Corrí*.) How do you say "green chili" (salsa verde)—the noun and adjective are reversed in Spanish. You need to learn these things, but that doesn't have to be hard. And even if you have it wrong, it will not stop you from communicating.

**EVEN IF YOU HAVE IT WRONG,
YOU CAN STILL COMMUNICATE.**

Grammar is good—but not critical. Let's get that straight first.

If I say to you: "Yesterday, I go to the beach. It is wonderful."

Not correct, but you know what I mean. And you can help me change it to, "Yesterday, I <u>went</u> to the beach. It <u>was</u> wonderful."

Improving your grammar can happen two ways: you can study, or you can listen and absorb. For children, it is all about the second option—your parents spoke to you, you learned. For adults, actually studying speeds up the process. We can often use logic to figure out how different parts of speech work together.

*If I had had time to go to the concert last night,*
*I would have had a chance to see One Republic.*

Compare to:

*If I were to go to the concert next month,*
*I would have a chance to see Chicago*
*(Best selling band in history—just sayin).*

For native speakers, it's usually pretty easy—but that's grammar, baby. Chances are, you didn't learn those kinds of constructions from your mom. You learned them in your high school or university English class. You *studied.*

For an immigrant to learn these phrases is just as daunting as it is for us to learn the same thing in a foreign language.

Still, this IS something you can do by yourself. Gradually. You can learn grammar rules and examples without having a private tutor. More importantly, you don't have to be able to make these constructions in order to be understood.

I know a lot of native English speakers who still can't make correct grammatical constructions. Maybe their family and community routinely use incorrect grammar and they have never changed—either because they don't want to put in the effort, or they just like their way better.

I am not even using perfect written grammar in this book! I do know what a complete sentence is, but you will see TONS of incomplete sentences here. Why? Because I hope you hear my voice—my message. I hope that, as you read, you *hear* these words, as if I were speaking you. (And for the autiobook – you ARE!)

Where/how can you improve these foundations? *Everywhere!*

There are hundreds, maybe thousands, of ways to build vocabulary and learn about grammar in a natural way—that is, by learning what sounds or looks right. And you can do this on your own.

Books, YouTube, Rosetta Stone, community college— all can help. Sales leaflets at Lowe's or Home Depot or other stores often have English and Spanish versions. Use all of these resources to pick up more vocabulary. As you gain exposure, you will pick up grammar aspects automatically. As with the example above: *Today I go to the beach. Yesterday I went to the beach. This month, I have gone to the beach three times. (Hoy, voy a la playa. Ayer, fui a la playa. Este mes, he ido a la playa tres veces.)*

## Practice:

The other thing you need in order to speak a new language is **practice**. So many people have said to me, "I used to be fluent... but I haven't practiced." That's the "use it or lose it" problem. But I like to say, "Use it or never have it!" If you don't have a chance to practice, all the vocabulary and grammar you are learning are just not going to "stick."

## Listening

- This should also be obvious. You can't have a conversation with someone—or know what they are even asking you—if you can't make out their words. *"What's your name? (¿Cómo te llamas?)"* or, *"Where are you from? (¿De dónde eres?)"* To do this, you have to "tune your ear" to the words and accents.

- This means you have to spend some time just listening. Even if you don't understand what the person is saying, you will begin to make out more and more individual words, and you can go look them up to build your vocabulary. You will also start picking up the grammar aspects from what the speakers are saying. I try to listen to something (radio, TV, YouTube) in Spanish for at least 15 minutes, twice a day.

This is in addition to any conversations I may have in Spanish during the day.

Where/how can you practice listening?

Well, again, the answer is—everywhere! On the Internet, especially YouTube; listen to the radio; watch TV (with subtitles, if available); join a meetup group for English/Spanish; at your work. Chances are, you work with a few Spanish speakers.

**Speaking**

- <u>This is the one area where you need someone else's help.</u> Let me say that again. ***You need a real, live, face-to-face person to really help you practice speaking***.

- Practicing in front of a mirror, or recording your voice and playing it back to yourself doesn't cut it. For this part, you need to practice with a person. Why? Because you need immediate feedback and positive reinforcement. Say you're teaching a kid to say hippopotamus or cinnamon. You can't just tell them to go practice on their own. It's not like throwing a baseball or dancing. They can't go practice 'til they get it right. It's a back-and-forth thing. They try to pronounce a word—you help them. They try again—you encourage them.

- Skype and other video chat options are better than nothing, but not nearly as effective as face-to-face. Why is that? Two reasons: First, when you are face-to-face, you can really SEE the other person's face and lips. They can SHOW you where their tongue is for certain sounds. And second, a big part of speaking a new language is confidence. Practicing over Skype doesn't have nearly the same benefits as practicing with a person in the same room as you.

**"If you want to learn to swim,**
**you have to get wet."**
**"You can't learn to ride a bike from a book."**

Where/how can you practice speaking?

Well, again, the answer is *everywhere*. But it's different.

So many people—English and Spanish speakers—say to me, "There isn't anyone I can practice with."

Well—for the Spanish speakers (learning English), I say—*You're in America*—of course there are English speakers you can practice with. If you need help finding them, let me know.

For the English speakers (learning Spanish), I say—*If you were to go to Spain, do you think there would be Spanish speakers?* The obvious reply is, "of course." Then I say—*The United States has more Spanish speakers than Spain!* If you need help finding them, let me know.

Spanish speakers make up 30 percent of our community here in Denver. In some neighborhoods, it's over 90 percent. Throughout the West and Southwest, you can easily find neighborhoods where more than half the people speak Spanish at home. And in just about every major population center, the percentage is at least 20 percent.

Spanish speakers are perhaps the most VISIBLE invisibles in the country. You see them at McDonalds, in your hotel, or up on your roof replacing the shingles. You see them or hear them in your school, at your hospital, at your church.

In fact, you probably run across native Spanish speakers every day. If you start to notice them and you want to learn Spanish, you may wish you could practice with them. But you hesitate. Because you're self-conscious and maybe feel it would be presumptuous to ask them to help you.

Guess what ... they really *want* to practice English with you. But they're not going to ask you to practice with them.

**YOU have to connect with THEM.**

It's a cultural thing. Americans often grow up with a "you can do anything" attitude. A support system. We have natural confidence (relative to many other cultures). In many other countries, confidence and self worth are not as built into the culture.

And they are immigrants! They are in an unfamiliar place.

If you are learning Spanish and are fortunate enough to be visiting or living in Colombia, picture how hard it would be to just walk up to someone and ask them to practice Spanish with you. This is even though you KNOW that the vast majority of them WANT to learn English.

Now imagine an immigrant here in the U.S., where they often think that most of us hate them (See Chapter 4 on stereotypes), and imagine how hard it would be for them to approach you to practice English.

I have seen it play out hundreds of times over the years at the ShareLingo Project. It's much, much harder for them to approach you—even if they are desperate to.

That's good for YOU—finding a practice partner is not as scary as you think it is.

Now imagine again that you're in Colombia, wanting to find someone to practice Spanish with, and then, like magic, a Colombian approaches you and says, "Hey. I'd love to practice English with you, and I can help you with your Spanish too. What do you think?" You would be excited, right? Maybe even grateful!

The good news is, here in the United States, if you just let Spanish speakers know you would like to practice Spanish and help them speak English, you will get their attention.

You don't even have to actually talk to someone in order to do that. You can just leave a flyer (in Spanish) with your contact information at your school or your work, offering to help them. Someone will contact you. I promise.

In fact—if you are school teacher—just send a flyer home with your students saying that you would like to practice English/Spanish with any parents that are interested in learning English. BOOM!

(If you want an Easy Button, check out The ShareLingo Project, which brings native speakers together to help each other.]

So—foundation and practice. That's the key. That's all it takes. I know that's all it takes because I've done it—rather, *I am doing it*. I'm learning more and more Spanish every day (I'm also learning more and more English every day—it never stops).

Whatever you do—keep it simple. Don't overthink it. The keys are **desire** and **being consistent**. You have to want it. And you have to commit to it.

Here is the main thing for you to remember!

## *NOTHING IS MORE EFFECTIVE FOR YOU TO LEARN SPANISH THAN HELPING SOMEONE LEARN ENGLISH.*

Why? The simple act of teaching English helps you think about and understand the words and phrases (in Spanish) that you are working with.

Learning by teaching is incredible. It's proven. It works.

# 8.0 How Does ShareLingo Work?

*By learning, you will teach.*
*By teaching, you will learn.*
*—Latin Proverb*

## 8.1 THE SHARELINGO MODEL

Your next question may be:

*Suppose I find a practice partner, or I set up a group in my company to practice together. What do I (we) do?*

This is the problem with the average language intercambio (or Meetup) group. There are some that work because they have a leader, but the vast majority don't have any structure.

After the first introduction, "Hello, my name is James," the "conversation" stalls. You stare at each other, get embarrassed, and move on to someone else. And it's probably someone else who speaks YOUR language.

I love Meetup. It's a great program for so many things— for finding people who like the same things you do, like hiking or sewing or whatever. I have not found them to be useful for language practice (speaking). And another issue with attending a language Meetup group is you may have to go halfway across town to attend it. It's far better if you can find a practice partner, or create a language group, in your neighborhood or your workplace.

Think of ShareLingo as "Language Outreach."

Rather than have a central school where everyone has to come and meet, we are much more interested in forming ShareLingo groups within communities. This can be in a church, community center, school, business, or just about any place that is large enough for the group to work well. If the weather is good, it can even be in a park.

The ShareLingo model brings small groups of English and Spanish speakers together to practice with each other. Generally, it's five to seven English speakers and an equal number of Spanish speakers. But the groups can be smaller or larger.

More recently, we have begun to provide the ShareLingo method and materials online, enabling the concept to expand further and faster than we can do it now, one class at a time. Even with the online version "www.iShareLingo.com," we focus on real people working together face-to-face. The "online" aspect is just a way for these participants to access the materials.

The most important thing is that there is a roughly even number of English and Spanish speakers. It can be as few as 1 English and 1 Spanish, or as many as 7 English and 7 Spanish. 10 people (5 each) seems to be the sweet spot. We don't recommend that groups get too much bigger than 10, because the whole point is for everyone to get to know and become friends with each other.

At ShareLingo, we provide a bilingual facilitator to keep things going smoothly, and we use our own materials, which are all written in a bilingual format. Almost any bilingual person can act as the facilitator. They just have to have a plan to work from.

When people from a community get together to teach each other, and they become friends, it has an additional impact—a ripple effect.

I'm standing in Sam's Club at the checkout line. I feel a tap on my shoulder and hear, "Mister James! How are you?" I turn and see Xavier (pronounced Hov-ee-air). He is a ShareLingo participant and is shopping with his family. He has a big smile on his face, and I am so pleased to see him. We talk for awhile, just pleasantries, really, but with great enthusiasm—*a friendship*—and then we part.

I could tell his family was curious about, "Who's that Gringo?" And the other people in the line, a mixture of Anglos and Latinos, were pretty curious about the interaction too. Xavier and I were bouncing back and forth between English and Spanish in the brief conversation. But everyone was smiling!

*Note: Xavier is in his 60s and he's a BRILLIANT stained glass artist. I've seen his work. He does some repair work occasionally. But due to language and other issues, he also works a couple of fast-food jobs to make ends meet. Sad, right? We're working on helping him with the language part so he can follow his passion.*

Xavier and his classmates in the ShareLingo class forged connections and friendships that extended into the community. And it had ripple effects. Xavier's family and those people standing in line at Sam's Club got to see and feel good about this connection between people from two different cultures.

We see this all the time at ShareLingo. By helping people in a local community center practice speaking with each other, it extends beyond the group. If two participants from different cultures accidentally bump into each other at the local grocery store or bank, they no longer ignore each other. They acknowledge each other. Maybe even hug. And the people around them see this.

When we work with a business to help their English and Spanish speakers understand each other, the relationships extend outside the classroom. When those participants see each other out in the field, on the shop floor, or in the hallways, they don't ignore each other. You hear, "Hola. ¿Cómo estás? Bien, Bien!"

## 8.2 THE SHARELINGO METHOD

**Each meeting, led by a facilitator,
is divided into three parts, or sessions.**

- In the first session (about 30 minutes), the group will review the previous class and preview this class's vocabulary.

- In the second session (about 1 hour), participants break up into pairs who help each other one-on-one. It's like having a private tutor.

- In the third session (about 30 minutes), the group gets back together to interact and solidify what was learned.

- Between meetings, the students have free access to an online platform where they can review additional materials for the course. Students are also encouraged to work with each other via phone, Facebook, Skype, FaceTime, etc., to reinforce the sessions.

These individual steps are really simple. But let's break them down a bit more.

## The first 30 minutes

In the first session, as a group, the participants "open up." We get them talking—in their native language, if that is more comfortable—or in their target language, if they want to try. We never put any pressure on anyone to "perform." During the first week, it is very common for people to start out very quiet. They don't know what to expect, because they have never seen anything like this before. They come into the ShareLingo group expecting it to be like the old-fashioned classroom they have experienced in the past.

Try to imagine—

Say your name is John or Jane. You're a native English speaker, but you want to practice Spanish. You want to do this for your job, or you want to travel, or maybe you want to meet somebody from a different culture. For whatever reason, you want to learn Spanish.

You've probably already tried a few things, like Duolingo or Rosetta Stone, or maybe even went to community college or university and studied Spanish. But you don't have a lot of confidence speaking Spanish, because you've never had an opportunity to practice with native speakers.

So if you come into a group of people—a combination of English and Spanish speakers—you might at first feel a little self-conscious about suddenly talking in Spanish. ShareLingo doesn't throw you under the bus like that. We might say, "Jane or John, how are you today?" And then you could tell us how you're doing today, even if it is in your native language. The benefit is that we are getting you to open up—to share something about yourself. And you're starting to talk. Meanwhile, the Spanish speakers in the room are getting to listen to your English.

Well if you, an English-speaking American, in America, are nervous that first day, imagine how an immigrant feels. They are, possibly for the first time, expected to speak in front of a group of Americans. Wow—that's scary.

So we say to Juan or Juana, "Cuéntanos, por favor, en español si prefieres, ¿Cómo estás hoy? (Tell us, please, in Spanish if you prefer, how are you today?)" And Juan or Juana will tell us how they are doing. They open up, and start talking in their own language. In Spanish.

You can see them visibly relax. Wait, I can talk in my own language? Chances are good that, in all of the ESL classes they have experienced, the teacher always made them talk in English ONLY. Most often, the teacher didn't speak a word of Spanish. And in all likelihood, the class was a mixture of people from Mexico, Japan, Honduras, Saudi Arabia, China, and other countries. All people wanting to learn English.

What's the problem? They're all learning English, right? Well, the problem is, the teacher—the sole native English speaker in the room—doesn't have time to practice with every person. So the students often have to practice with each other. Imagine trying to learn French and practicing with someone from Russia, Singapore, or Germany who was also trying to learn French. Talk about negative reinforcement!

In a beginner-level class, the English speakers probably do not know what the Spanish speakers are saying. And the Spanish speakers do not know what the English speakers are saying to each other. But they hear a little bit of their target language, and they get to understand it's okay to talk even if you are not understood. Because there are other people in the room in the same situation. As the weeks go by, everyone becomes friends. There is trust.

Next, as a group, we go over last week's materials to see if there are any questions. If there was homework assigned, then we review that. Next, we go over this week's vocabulary, and each person has an opportunity to practice the words and phrases for the lesson for this week. This gives everyone a chance to get comfortable with, and ask questions about, the materials they are about to work with.

## The next hour

The next step of the process is where the magic of the ShareLingo experience actually happens. This is when the group breaks up into pairs: one English speaker and one Spanish speaker. Together. Maria reads a little to me in Spanish. Then I read the same thing, in Spanish, and she helps me with pronunciation. Then I read the same thing in English, and when Maria reads in English, I help her. We go back and forth, back and forth. We are constantly changing from learner to helper and back.

These 60 minutes pass quickly. Unbelievably quickly. It feels like it's just 10 or 15 minutes.

Psychologically, your mind is accustomed to NOT focusing on any one thing for long periods of time. It has to do with survival. If you're being hunted by bears, lions, or dinosaurs, it makes sense to look up and check your surroundings once in awhile. This is why, when you are in math or history class, you start to get distracted after a few minutes. Your brain loses focus on what is going on at the front of the class and wants to check out other things. Since there ARE no other things, you get bored.

But when you are switching from teacher to student to teacher to student, your brain doesn't know you're doing the same thing. Your "look up and check for danger" clock keeps getting reset. Time flies.

During these 60-or-so minutes (it's often hard to break up the pairs and drag them back to the group), we actually encourage the pairs to "go off on tangents." For example, if the materials are talking about Christmas, it may start a conversation about what Christmas is like in the different cultures. That may lead to what Halloween, or Día de los Muertos, is all about. (It's NOT the same thing, even though it falls at same time—within a day of each other.) Sometimes the pair spends the bulk of the time talking to each other and not going over the materials. THAT'S SUCCESS!!

Our goal is not to "get through the textbook." Our goal is to help two people, from different cultures, connect with each other.

The focus during this time is so great, so intense, that everything else drops off and becomes insignificant. This is HUGE. Because this is where the cultural acceptance part of our program really takes place.

When little Juana from El Salvador steps foot into the first class, she may be terrified. She's doing it anyway, because she wants to speak English and get ahead. But it is no less daunting. She's paired with, say, Linda, someone who WANTS to speak Spanish. Linda is, almost by definition, someone accepting of Juana.

In just a few seconds, as Juana learns a little from Linda and then starts TEACHING Linda, something amazing happens. Juana feels her self-worth. She feels important. Each time she offers Linda corrections (something she may NEVER do in another setting), she feels intelligent. And Linda is THANKING her for the corrections. When the roles are reversed, and Linda corrects Juana, it is no longer something negative. It is positive. Juana is grateful for the help, not self-conscious about the correction.

This experience is different from any previous language-learning experience the participants may have had, where everything was difficult, negative, and disheartening.

During this time, when Juana is helping Linda learn Spanish, do you think Linda cares what COLOR Juana is? Does Linda cares if Juana is gay, Catholic, or handicapped? Does Linda care what kind of job or how much education Juana has? Does Linda care if Juana drives a fancy car?

Nope—none of that. What Linda cares about is that Juana is a native Spanish speaker, willing to help Linda achieve her goal of learning and speaking Spanish. Period.

Does Juana care if Linda is black, white, a nurse, or a police officer? Nope. She may be INTERESTED in Linda, but she won't be judging.

In one of our classes, the facilitator was a man named Abram. Abram spent several years in Chile, where he met his partner, Lorenzo. Lorenzo attended the ShareLingo class that Abram was facilitating so that he could practice speaking English with someone besides Abram. They always spoke Spanish at home, because it was easier.

Mike and Diana are two Christian missionaries (great people) who were learning Spanish to prepare for a mission trip to (I believe) Guatemala.

On this day, Diana and Lorenzo happened to be working with each other. On this day, the topic was "family tree," and of course one part of that was wife/husband, along with brother-in-law, niece, aunt, etc. Now, Lorenzo is a hoot. He's artistic, theatrical, a dancer, and an extrovert. Diana couldn't be more different. She is a wonderful person (most missionaries are, right?), but conservative. Quiet. Focused. You might say, mission oriented.

Lorenzo kept saying, "My husband did this, and my husband did that." Diana kept trying to correct him. My WIFE did this, my WIFE did that. Diana thought Lorenzo was just confused with the English. But Lorenzo was insistent. No, my HUSBAND.

I was listening.

I finally said, "Diana, he's correct. He means his husband."

She looked at me. It took her a moment to process. Clearly, I knew the difference between "wife" and "husband." And it was sinking in.

The light went on. The gavel dropped. The cannon went off. BOOM. She got it.

Lorenzo has a HUSBAND.

I think he may be the first out-front gay person Diana ever spoke with.

And then, she said, "OHHHH."

And off they went. Back to practicing, laughing, and smiling. Helping each other.

Now, we need to make sure the participants don't spend the whole time working on pronunciation, which is tempting. They make such amazing progress with pronunciation, the thing that may be the biggest hurdle for them, that they can forget to work on another aspect of the ShareLingo model—comprehension.

The part of your brain that does pronunciation is not the same part that works on comprehension. Pronunciation is more of a muscular thing—like hitting a baseball. Can you get your muscles to do what you want them to? Anybody who has tried to take up golf at a later age can attest to how difficult that can be.

Comprehension, on the other hand, is part of the language center of your brain. It has to be exercised also, or you won't remember any new words. I'll speak about

ShareLingo materials in the next section, but for now just know that all of our materials are written in a format that lets the participants cover (hide) either the English or Spanish portion. One of the exercises we get everyone to practice is to cover one side (English or Spanish) and translate the words and phrases. The practice partner helps with this process so that nobody is lost or frustrated with this exercise. This "translation" period is what activates that language center in the brain.

## The last 30 minutes

Debrief. Decompress.

Wow—it's like you just did an hour, non-stop, on the StairMaster at the gym.

You were engaged the whole time. Focused. Excited. You were "in the zone." Runner's high.

Take a moment to breathe. Relax.

This is the time we reinforce a few things, while letting other things sink in. It's also a time for the group to discuss and collaborate on what may have been difficult.

But this is also when everyone is jazzed, so it's normally the noisiest time. Everyone wants to talk. To share. People talk about what they learned with each other. And they feed off each other. They find out that they are not the only ones that had problems with a word, or phrase.

The facilitator is there to document what's happening; for example, to write all the difficult words on a whiteboard.

But mostly, it is still about the group helping each other. Our facilitators don't really teach English or Spanish—though they may explain concepts sometimes. They are there to help the participants teach each other.

You may think the materials would be a critical component of this process. The truth is, while the format and the level of the materials are important, the actual content of the materials is not very important.

Well, not very important to the PROCESS.

Let's talk about materials next.

## 8.3 THE SHARELINGO (OR OTHER) MATERIALS

Content and level. That's what's important. Which one is MOST important?

One of the problems I see with university courses, Rosetta Stone, DuoLingo, and other learning methods is that in many aspects they are "one size fits all." Don't get me wrong, I think these are all great programs. Duolingo is a really, really great program that we recommend to every ShareLingo student starting out. Yes, there are some generic things that everyone has to learn. Like, everyone wants to know how to say "good morning" and "good afternoon," regardless if they are a nurse, school teacher, or missionary.

But by far the most common reason we hear for why people want to learn a language is "for work."—To be better at their job, to earn higher pay, or to get a new job.

Therefore, at ShareLingo, we structure materials to the participants. We don't have the same materials, for example, for nurses, as we do for school teachers. All of the materials will include the basics, like "good morning," but for nurses, we might practice, "How is your blood pressure?" And for teachers, we might go over, "Please, for the love of GOD, sit down and be quiet."

ALL of our materials are created in a bilingual, side-by-side, format.

| INTRODUCING YOURSELF | PRESENTÁNDOTE |
|---|---|
| **CONVERSATION ONE** | **CONVERSACIÓN UNO** |
| 1. Good morning. | 1. Buenos días. |
| 2. Hello. | 2. Hola. |
| 3. Nice to meet you. I am _____. | 3. Mucho gusto. Me llamo _____. |
| 4. My name is _____. Nice to meet you. | 4. Mi nombre es _____. Es un placer conocerte. |

What would happen if a school teacher did our course for nurses? Well, a lot. Do you think a teacher might want to know how to say, "blood pressure"? Probably. It's not wasted time.

But if you are just starting to learn Spanish, you might be overwhelmed with a lesson that teaches: "If I were to go to the beach tomorrow, I might see a dolphin." Similarly, if you are at an intermediate or advanced level already, and we are practicing "uno, dos, tres" (one, two, three), you might get a little bored and frustrated.

What we have found is that level is much more important than content. We try to match speakers together who are at about the same level. This is not because of ability. It is because of interest. As a native English speaker, I can "come up" to whatever level an immigrant needs. And for me learning Spanish, they can "come down" to whatever level I need. But if one person has to "come down" to another person's level, they get bored. And the "teaching" becomes one-sided. The more advanced person tends to teach the less advanced.

In international language learning, there are certain very specific, very defined, levels.

*See this Wiki for more information on these standards:*
*http://bit.ly/BWResource10*

Because we are focused on conversation and friendship more than how many words you learn, ShareLingo has a comparatively simple four-level structure:

- Beginner—never ever had any exposure to the new language but wants to learn.

- Basic—Some exposure, like high school. Can probably do the alphabet, colors, etc., but other than that, they are starting from scratch. Everything is in the present tense, and the most focus is on first and second person—*Where do YOU work? I work at Starbucks.*

- Intermediate—Ready for other tenses: past, present, conditional, etc. We help people learn, for example, that in Spanish, there are two different types of past tense!

- Advanced—Free thought and conversation. This is not to say unguided. We still use materials and a method. But here, the participants practice how to describe FEELINGS.


Remember, we are focused more on speaking than anything else. Once we have established levels, we can create a class and match up participants.

From here, there are several options for the materials we use:

- Generic materials we have already created.

  - *Good morning; my name is; etc.*

- Generic materials for a specific industry.

  - *Where does it hurt?; We are working on decimals; A hard hat is required.*

- Specific materials for an organization.

  - Custom designed prior to beginning of classes. For example:

    - A bank may not just want generic banking material, but material that includes their specific products and services.

    - A hotel may not want generic hospitality material, but material that includes specific information about their property. Every participant will practice all of the phrases that are important on that property.

    - A construction company may not want generic safety information, but safety information relating specifically to whatever their insurance company requires.

- Dual-language books, or books that have already been translated into many languages.

  - *The Alchemist*—Paulo Cuelo

  - *The Bible*—God

- Bilingual business material.

  - For example, The Matos Law Firm here has information available for both English and Spanish speakers about what to do in the event of a car accident. This type of material teaches something important at the same time that we use it to practice language.

- And the participants' own material.

    o In every class, participants are encouraged to bring their own words and phrases and have the class help translate and practice them. Even though these materials are inherently specific to one person's needs, the entire class nearly always benefits.

The final example above is BIG. It is SO big that it could form the basis of our entire program. Or YOUR entire program. Once we teach two people how to effectively practice together, they can use ANY materials. Why not have them work with what is specifically important to them—in their job, for their family, to travel, or whatever?

The important thing that I will say again and again and again is that the two people gain *trust* for each other. It is the *trust* that allows an open conversation. They feel as if they can ask each other anything, and really, they CAN!

**Warning—bad words follow…**

The English language has sounds that the Spanish language simply doesn't have. Vowels in Spanish always sound the same.

|   |     |
|---|-----|
| A | ah  |
| E | ay  |
| I | ee  |
| O | oh  |
| U | oo  |

Compare that to English

|   |              |
|---|--------------|
| A | Bake, Back   |
| E | Bead, Bed    |
| I | Bite, Bit    |
| O | Boat, Bottle |
| U | Bute, But    |

What does this have to do with bad words?

Well, sometimes Spanish speakers literally can not hear the difference between

*Beach* and *Bitch*

***or***

*Sheet* and *Shit*

I know someone who has been here for many years and is completely fluent. But she's not a native speaker. And she will still not say "a sheet of paper." She says, "A piece of paper," because she has such bad memories (of being laughed AT) from when she was first learning.

We have to help the English learners. We have to let them see and hear, and sometimes feel, how we pronounce different words.

This is one benefit of the ShareLingo model.

It's safe.

People trust each other. Even to the point of asking about something that might be embarrassing in other settings.

And when they get to this point, it opens the door to real conversations about all kinds of other things. Like religion, politics, and sexuality.

**Think about what kind of materials you could create, or that you may already have, that could be used in a group like this. Even if the materials are not already bilingual, but they relate to the concepts that need to be conveyed in your setting, they can form the basis of a ShareLingo style class.**

# 9.0 Conclusion

*There is no wilderness like a life without friends;
friendship multiplies blessings and minimizes
misfortunes; it is a unique remedy against
adversity, and soothes the soul.*
*—Baltasar Gracián*

World Peace—that's the ultimate goal with this book. It has to do with the idea that everyone can be friends, and that starting a conversation by sharing languages can start the process.

Thank you so much for reading this book. But more importantly, I hope that you will implement a ShareLingo-style program within your organization. Be that company, church, school, community center, nonprofit—or just a group of neighbors. I know you will see friendships develop and strengthen.

Not only will you or your company benefit by achieving your goals for language acquisition or a healthier bottom line, but you will also help our immigrant community navigate our often complex and sometimes daunting society.

EMPATHY AND RESPECT
*http://bit.ly/BWVideo8*

# ACKNOWLEDGMENTS

This book would not have been possible without the help, patience, input, and participation of so very many people.

THANK YOU, **Rocío del Pilar Durán**. If anyone in the world can be considered ShareLingo's "co-founder," it is you. Although you are moving on to follow your own dreams, desires, and calling, your help building ShareLingo has been invaluable in so many ways— marketing, outreach, training, and most importantly, helping with product development. Rocío, you have been my ShareLingo practice partner—we have helped each other practice and speak English and Spanish, and much of the model is based on our experiences working together.

THANK YOU to the many, many **ShareLingo participants** (both English and Spanish speakers) who have attended and supported the program—and especially the ones from the early days, when we didn't have a clue what we were doing. I also want to thank the many bilingual facilitators who have helped so many of these students excel. In particular, **Nicole Dalby,** who helped with the very first class for the very first ShareLingo group. **Diana Cortez, Abram Palmer,** and **Danny Mejia** have each facilitated multiple groups in multiple locations, and have helped a great deal in improving the model and materials. And there are many others.

THANK YOU to the many people who contributed their stories, quotes, and insights as I was writing Beyond Words.

THANK YOU to all the people who have helped me turn this idea into an actual book. These include the members of the SPS Mastermind Community, as well as **Ray Brehm** of Bestseller University—who was instrumental in helping with all the Kindle, Amazon, and Launch "stuff" that turned out to be my biggest hurdle. Thanks, **Derek Bearman**, for the proofreading, as well as sharing your story. And a HUGE thanks to **Mr. Steve Krizman**, who "worked like a burro" alongside me on editing, prioritizing, and even filling in many blanks.

THANK YOU, **Simon Page**, for handling all the tech—website, Facebook, clickfunnels, and the GRAPHICS (Simon did the *Beyond Words* cover design). What you do is an ART, and you are so freakin' good at it.

THANK YOU, **Ana Ugarte**, my "Virtual Assistant", and so much more, in Nicaragua. Ana—you've helped me in so many ways to not go crazy in the short time since we connected.

THANK YOU, **Faeizah Rajimin**. You have encouraged me and helped me through a long and stressful transition period in my life. You have the patience of Job.

**Muchísimas Gracias a Todos**

# ABOUT THE AUTHOR

*In the end, it's not about you,*
*and it's not about me. It's about us.*
*—Pinterest*

You can totally skip this section. I included it because people told me I had to so that you, if you choose, can get to "know" me.

I think the next section, How ShareLingo Started, is far more interesting.

I took Spanish in High School, just like millions of other people. And, just like for millions of other people, it didn't work. At least it didn't work well. I did the same, "¿Dónde está la biblioteca?" that everyone did. I tried to memorize the verb tenses. Mostly, they didn't sink in.

My dad was in the Air Force, and during my senior year in high school, we moved to Italy. I know. Rough life. I used to skip classes on Fridays and go to Venice by train.

What I found was that I could somehow communicate with the Italians. A little Italian, a little Spanish, a little English, and a few hand signals. By just *trying*, I ended up *doing*. And I loved it.

But, you know, it was my senior year. And in high school, they give you an aptitude test, and then tell you what you should be "when you grow up." They told me to be an engineer, and off I went to college (Iowa State—go Cyclones) and became a computer engineer (that's like an electrical engineer, but with more programming, and back in the early '80s when I did it, it was a very new field of study).

The thing is, I wasn't encouraged to follow my passion for people and languages. In fact, I was *DIS*couraged from doing so. Even though I loved the cultural experience in Italy, I was pretty geeky. I didn't have great social skills. That aptitude test suggested, among other things, that I wasn't very good with real people, so I didn't follow the inner dream.

My dad was my hero, so don't take this wrong. It wasn't that he wasn't supportive. It was a different time. He felt he was looking out for my best interest by steering me away from the humanities and into engineering. I nearly dropped out of school a few times—not for grades, and not because I partied too much, but just because I didn't like it. I wanted to go drive a truck or join the peace corps or something. But my dad would talk me down. Straighten me out. And I made it. I graduated.

I became an engineer for McDonnell Douglas back in the '80s—putting in large computer systems for the F18 military jet project. First, they sent me to Canada for a year.

Cold Lake, Alberta, Canada. There's a military base there, and that's where I worked for a year with McDonnell Douglas. In the summer, the days are 23 hours long. The fishing and outdoor life is spectacular. In the winter, the nights are 23 hours long. The ice on the lake gets to 4 or 5 feet thick. You need to put an extension on your ice auger to go ice fishing. The people form a wonderful, tight-knit community: a mixture of English and French speakers with hockey as a common bond.

Then to Australia, for what was supposed to be another one-year assignment.

While in Australia, I married, had two beautiful kids, and left McDonnell to work for a conference and exhibition company. Over the following 9 years, I worked my way up from computer programmer to director and general manager of the company. I did my MBA in international finance. The business grew enormously. I lived an "executive" lifestyle. Perfect life, right? Perfect thin blonde wife. Two kids—boy, girl, three years apart, attending private schools. Weekends out on Sydney Harbour on my father-in-law's massive boat. I golfed. A lot.

But I gave all that up.

I dreamed about starting my own business. Something that could help people.

In 1994, leaving a "great job" and nearly all my "wealth" behind, I brought my family to the United States to basically start over. I purchased an art gallery in Breckenridge, Colorado. I didn't know anything about owning a gallery, but hey, how hard can it be, right? And HEY, it's Breckenridge! Well, it was hard. My wife went from no job to a 14-hour-a-day job. (She wasn't that impressed with the idea). We just couldn't get reliable staff in that small ski town, and our kids didn't fit in as well in school there. So, the lifestyle didn't fit our family, and we only owned the art gallery for one year.

But we sold the gallery for twice what we paid for it. How? Well, when I bought the gallery, all the records were handwritten on index cards. I wrote a software program to manage everything. When we sold the business, the new owners had very detailed records about what was selling, where all the inventory was, what was on consignment, etc.

> Looking back, owning that gallery was a blessing for me for two important reasons: I learned how to talk to people (and learned that I like it), and I wrote that software program. It's been upgraded many times now and is still used in galleries around the world. Even when I look at the latest generation, I can see the bones of that original version I started over 20 years ago. It was good code.
>
> When people came into the gallery, I found that I could talk to them. Easily. I wasn't so much selling as asking what they were looking for. But many of those conversations turned into sales.

We sold the gallery a year after we bought it to "save the marriage." So, for a "job," I started getting that software ready for other galleries to buy.

I was living in Breckenridge. I coached Little League. I golfed and skied; not a lot, but whenever I could.

I could have done it for the rest of my life. But, again, family circumstances steered me in a different direction. My wife was Australian. She was having a hard time adapting to the culture of a small American ski town. The schools in Breckenridge, at least at that time, were not what we were looking for. I'll leave it at that.

We moved down to the Denver area in 1997. Better schools. Warmer. Better for the software business.

I improved the software and sold it to art galleries and antique dealers all over the world. I built a huge database of art by combining all the online art from all of the galleries that had my system. I loved talking to all the people. Cool, right? We were making a pretty good living. We didn't want for anything important. But it was hard.

In 2008, we sold that business as well. I "retired young." We joined a country club. I played golf and tennis. My wife was in her element; I was not.

I didn't like the people around me. And I was bored.

To keep occupied, I invented a silicone kitchen gadget. I did all the design and prototyping. I got it manufactured (in China, sadly, because you just can't get that kind of thing made here at a price you can sell it). But I made it, and we took it to market.

I was still playing golf and tennis. And I was still lacking something.

When people asked what I did for a living, I never said I was "retired." I would say, "I'm looking for a new opportunity." Truth is, I hope I don't ever really retire. I hope I can keep working until I drop dead. I love what I do now. But at that time, I was not happy.

### I was looking for a *purpose.*

I kept coming back to the idea from long ago that I wanted to learn a language.

That dream that I had never followed.

And then—ShareLingo.

Follow James on:
Linkedin at https://www.linkedin.com/in/jbarcherjr/
And his blog at www.archer.com.

# II. How ShareLingo Started

*Every great dream begins with a dreamer.*
*Always remember, you have within you the*
*strength, the patience, and the passion to*
*reach for the stars to change the world.*
*—Harriet Tubman*

ShareLingo started when I was trying to learn Spanish. I was 54. (You don't have to be a teenager to learn a language.)

I considered learning Italian. I think Italian and French are just incredibly sexy, and I had a little bit of a head start with Italian from all those years ago (see the previous section). But I live in Denver. And I'm an engineer, remember. So I decided that Spanish was a lot more practical for me—something that I now think is one of the best decisions of my life.

I did everything: I tried CDs, books, and Rosetta Stone; I went to Costa Rica and attended four different language schools; Grammar, Grammar, Grammar.

I just wanted to TALK.

Like so many people tell me about their trips to language schools, I gained more confidence in speaking Spanish from the people I was staying with than in the schools I attended.

When I got back to Denver, I wanted to practice Spanish. But it was hard, even for me, to just walk up to someone and ask if they would practice. So I volunteered to teach ESL (English as a Second Language) at a place called Centro San Juan Diego—it's the Catholic Hispanic outreach center here in Denver.

What was different about me, compared to the other "teachers", was—

1. I am white.

2. I wasn't a teacher.

3. I wasn't there to TEACH them.

4. I was there to LEARN from them.


In my class, I made it very clear, right away, that we were there to help each other.

That changed everything.

It opened up *real* conversations. They could ask me ANYTHING, and I learned about them and their stories too. Where they worked. Where they came from. How they came to Denver. I'm still friends with many of those first students.

That was the first "Ah ha" moment. Instead of teaching English in one room and Spanish in another room, wouldn't it be great if English and Spanish speakers could learn at the same time—from each other?

I looked for a program I could join to do that. It didn't exist. There were Meetup groups and Intercambios. But in the Meetup groups I attended, it was normally seven or eight English speakers trying to speak Spanish to each other. In the few groups that did have native Spanish speakers, they talked to each other, and the English speakers (me included) were just overwhelmed and lost. Intercambios, I've found, are often more about the beer and dating than an exchange of language.

So, since it didn't exist, and almost by accident, I started The ShareLingo Project. It didn't start as a "business." I found a nonprofit near me that had a classroom I could borrow (Thank you, Jeffco Action Center). I put up flyers at Starbucks and a few other places to find people who wanted to learn Spanish. I went to local places like Chipotle where Spanish speakers were working to find people who wanted to learn English.

The program I put together was free.

And it worked. It didn't work because of me. It worked in spite of me.

I was unorganized. I didn't have good materials. I didn't have a lesson plan. I gave them all a copy of a friend's bilingual children's book (Thank you, Karen Rowan, for letting me use your materials), and asked them to read to and speak with each other. The ages in that group ranged from 15 to 80 years old.

It was the coolest thing ever. It went on for several weeks, and towards the end, all the English speakers were invited to a quinceañera [Keens - on - yer - ah]. That's the Latino version of a Sweet Sixteen party, but for 15-year-olds—and it's a big deal. All of us "white folks" were so grateful to be there, but we were treated as guests of honor when we arrived that day. We had a great time!

I think it was right at that moment that I found my mission in life.

I could help connect people and break down cultural barriers.


OK—so, I had an idea that a program like this could work. But it needed more organizing. Better materials. And, the big question: Would anyone pay for it?

I thought about forming ShareLingo as a nonprofit. But I've been on several nonprofit boards and I can tell you that the way we treat nonprofits in this country is stupid. We make it almost impossible for them to survive and excel. We make the people who work there earn less money, and God forbid they actually advertise to get more customers.

> Watch fundraiser **Dan Pallotta** describe our messed up model for charities: they are rewarded for how little they spend, not for what they accomplish. (https://youtu.be/bfAzi6D5FpM)

Then I found the Social Enterprise model. To be precise, I found Tom's Shoes, that amazing company that has helped millions of people get shoes, eyeglasses, and other services. They have been able to do this because they have a revenue model. They make enough money themselves to follow their mission. They don't ask for grants. My feeling is that the main reason they are so successful and help so many people, is because they are NOT a nonprofit.

Bingo.

Then, God sent me Rocío Durán, an amazing woman from Colombia, who was able to help me develop the materials. Over the following three years, we tuned and honed the method and materials that are in use now. The method, by the way, is much more important than the materials.

With ShareLingo, I want to be able to provide the services to schools, nonprofits, and other social causes for free. But it has to be self-sustaining. I put in all the seed money, but it needs to make its own money in order to grow. So I started charging businesses I help for language and diversity training. It's still cheap, because it's about the mission. But they pay. I also charge individuals who want to do the course on their own (though, that's at half the business rate).

And I'm writing this book.

And I'm branching out into an online version so people outside of Denver can use the ShareLingo method and materials.

I digress.

In the three-plus years developing this program, we have seen a very diverse group of people come together and help each other. We have worked with schools, lawyers, and police. We've worked with the LGBTQ community, the YMCA, and churches.

And it's *working*.

It seems to be what everyone needs.

My dream—my vision, if you will—is to help a million people all over the world learn a second language and experience other cultures. Even if they do this in their own backyard.

Thank you, again and again, for being a part of this dream.

The mission of The ShareLingo Project is to improve cultural understanding and acceptance by leveraging language learning as common ground to bring cultures together for the benefit of the participants, their families, their employers, their communities, and our society.

*We support understanding and respect*
*between people from different cultures.*

The ShareLingo Project believes that shared language learning can eliminate the bias and fear between people from different cultures.

*We will help millions of people talk to each other*
*and stop being so afraid of one another.*

# III. If I Didn't Speak Spanish, I Would Have Missed a Great Opportunity.

(Fall, 2016)  http://bit.ly/BWResource14

Hi, Everyone—I'M IN COLOMBIA! And no, folks—they *don't* speak English everywhere.

Lots of Americans believe that wherever they go, people will speak English. In the past couple of months, I've been to England, France, Italy, and now Colombia. I can tell you that's not the case at all (other than England, obviously... Duh). [The Europe experience is a different story—that was all pleasure, with no "business objectives."]

This month, I am in Medellin Colombia to check out whether there is potential for The ShareLingo Project* to help the people down here. So, even though I'm looking forward to the personal side of this trip and getting to know Medellin, I'm here for business.

I arrived on Thursday, and had a great chat with the cab driver on the 40-minute ride from the airport down into town—who, guess what, didn't speak any English except "Taxi, Taxi?" (we worked on that—he's much better with the "Would you like a taxi?" phrase now...).

But the next day, Friday, I was fortunate to be able to attend a speed-networking event hosted by a new coworking space here called Siembra (which means sow, or sowing, as in seeds).

It was an amazing meeting with about 30 participants that ranged from lawyers, to web designers, to Social Entrepreneurs, plus the hosts (Al and Mala), of course. Within that group, there were a few who spoke English—including two or three from the U.K. But I think I was the only American (though one of the Colombians did grow up in Miami) and many of the people spoke little or no English at all. But I really wanted to meet them all—because they were young, and passionate, and ready to change the world. It was very exciting.

The thing about speed networking is you change partners every few minutes. People move from table 1, to 2, to 3, etc, so I didn't have the option of only talking to people who spoke English and just hanging out with them. Thanks to ShareLingo, my Spanish is pretty good. In fact, it was good enough to have great conversations with everyone as we changed partners.

I met a great lawyer that helps startups navigate the Colombian requirements. I met a great accountant that helps startups as well (every business here that isn't a personal business has to have an accountant.)

And I made some great contacts who we may be able to partner with in one capacity or another down here for web design, creating a mobile app, etc. I'm also pleased that pretty much everyone in the room was excited about what ShareLingo does, and could personally relate to how much it's needed. Especially the ones that don't speak

English yet and know they need to. Not only was this networking, it was market research!

I COULD NOT HAVE DONE SO MUCH IN ONE EVENING WITHOUT SPANISH. PERIOD.
It would have been a great opportunity lost.

Also on this trip, I've managed to find a lot of great restaurants and places to shop. I picked up some new polo shirts, complete with ShareLingo logos, for about $6 each. I've purchased clothes and shoes. And I have found out where to find printing, and stationery, and lots of other services. I even went to church. All in Spanish. And all in just a couple of days. NONE of the shop keepers I worked with spoke English.

So if you are thinking about working with any of the Central or South American countries—or, indeed, if you're thinking about working with the Hispanic community in the U.S., you owe it to yourself to make the effort to learn Spanish before you go. And you can— believe me. I was over 50 when I started learning Spanish. I know that anyone can do it. Start with Duolingo or another program to learn some vocabulary and get your feet under you (Pimsleur actually gave me the best head start) and then find a practice partner, through ShareLingo, of course!!

You will be so glad you did. And you won't miss out on lots of great opportunities as you travel!

*The ShareLingo Project is a Social Enterprise that helps English and Spanish speakers come together and teach each other—face-to-face—to help break down cultural barriers.

# IV. — Should I Still Learn Spanish?

With Trump's win, should you still learn Spanish?

http://bit.ly/BWResource15

Yes; now more than ever.

The results of the elections this week surprised many people and communities. Many immigrants and their families are scared. Children in schools are crying because they don't understand the fear their parents are feeling, or they are being bullied simply because they are Latino. This is not just among the undocumented. And it's not just the Hispanic community that is affected. New immigrants in general are worried about America's feelings toward their presence in this country. They are genuinely afraid of an uprising and backlash against them.

I happen to be in Colombia this month, and the feeling here is also one of fear and puzzlement. How could this happen?

The answer, in my mind, is that the discord and division within our country has reached a crisis level, and it's not just the new immigrants who are scared. The fear is on BOTH sides.

Working-class white and black people are also scared. They are afraid for the economy. For their jobs.

For their future.

But we can't let this fear, on both sides, drive us further into division. Our country was founded upon a great immigration ideal. I know I share this sentiment with lots of people.

So how can we take steps to come together?

There are hundreds, if not thousands, of posts today about getting along. I do want to echo those sentiments, but with a different approach.

One way to address some of the tension and misunderstanding is through language. Actually, language learning. Now more than ever, it is important for the immigrant community to learn English. But it is also important for more and more people to learn Spanish and other languages.

Why?

Because we must live and work together. The present fear and misunderstandings can have no positive effect within communities and corporations. Sharing language is the most powerful way to break down barriers that we have.

Even prior to the elections, many companies were experiencing tension between their English- and non-English-speaking leaders and workers. The ShareLingo Project has been working with some of these companies in Denver to help correct that situation and improve the work culture within them. Put simply, we help English and Spanish speakers communicate with each other about their work goals and objectives, and their cultural values. And it's an effective program.

So what about you? If you were thinking about learning Spanish prior to the elections, why was that? Do you feel any of your prior motivations have changed? I doubt it.

For example, if you are a nurse, or pastor, or nonprofit manager who works with non-English speakers, has your mission changed? If you are a salesperson who is trying to access the $1.6 trillion Hispanic market in the US, has that changed? If you are someone who wants to travel and experience the world, has that changed? If you are the CEO of a manufacturing, construction, landscaping, or service business who wants your company to be as efficient and productive as possible, has that changed?

No.

Now more than ever, I feel that we must take steps to learn about other languages and cultures. And while I tend to focus on Spanish, because that's what MY social enterprise is working on, I believe it applies equally to ALL languages and cultures.

I'm not fond of the phrase "Make America Great Again" because I happen to believe it never stopped being great. But I also believe we can be greater. That is, if we can get through divisiveness and work and pull together.

Whether you are White, Brown, Yellow, or Black; Christian, Muslim, or Jew; Gay, Straight, or Trans— Please, today, every time you encounter someone from another culture, reach out to them with a nod, or a smile, or a handshake. Let them know that you want us to be united, and not divided.

Or even better—say *Bienvenido*.

# V. Mara's Story

## Uniendo Comunidades Rompiendo Barreras

Con frecuencia se escucha que "Estados Unidos es el país de las oportunidades, y que si uno está dispuesto a trabajar duro, logrará sus sueños." Pero de lo que no se habla, y que tiene un gran impacto en nuestro camino al éxito, es de la importancia de integrarse a una nueva cultura. Desde la comida y el idioma hasta la forma de pasar el tiempo libre son diferentes a las de nuestro país de origen. Yo soy Mexicana, y a pesar de que hay muchos Mexicanos en el estado de Colorado, el shock cultural que viví una vez que llegue a éste país fue muy grande e intimidante.

Sin embargo, si has emigrado a los Estados Unidos en busca del tan anhenlado "Sueño Americano," probablemente has notado cómo nuestra comunidad inmigrante tiende a alejarse de la cultura Americana.

Aún recuerdo el terror que me daba el tener que ir a un súper mercado Americano, donde, por supuesto, la gente no hablaba español. Y la frustración al sentir que no podía ordenar en un restaurante de comida rápida. La barrera del idioma era enorme. Así que, para no sentirme inútil, hacia todo lo que necesitaba en español. Para mi suerte, encontrar súper mercados y restaurantes Latinos aquí en Denver es bastante fácil.

El tiempo fue pasando, y poco a poco, me di cuenta que, a pesar de que uno, sí, puede sobrevivir en éste país sin hablar el idioma, la pérdida por no involucrarse en la cultura Americana es basta e irreversible, desde conocer a gente nueva, hacer una llamada telefónica, asistir a una conferencia, o escuchar la música del momento, hasta conversar con mis maestros. Todo esto me ayudó a comprender que, para alcanzar el "Sueño Americano," necesitaba incluirme en la cultura, y por supuesto, dominar el inglés.

Una vez que decidí enfocarme y aprender inglés lo mejor posible, noté que mi lista de opciones se extendío. Es así como ir a cualquier súper mercado, cine, restaurante, e iglesia, hasta mi manera de pensar se expandieron poco a poco. Ahora tengo la oportunidad de realizar todas esas actividades sin pena por no saber comunicarme en otro idioma. Ya no siento miedo al ordenar una hamburguesa con papas fritas, al igual que me siento capaz de ir a un banco y hacer una transacción. Por el contrario, aprender inglés ha aumentado mi nivel de confianza en mí misma. Y me ha dado la seguridad para sentir que yo también pertenezco a éste país como cualquier otra persona.

El Proyecto ShareLingo existe porque desea que nuestra comunidad inmigrante saque provecho de todas las oportunidades que hay en éste país. Que dejemos de excluirnos y segregarnos a nosotros mismos. La misión de ShareLingo es que las comunidades Anglosajonas y Latinas se unan a través del idioma, que los Americanos aprendan español, así como los Latinos inglés. Ellos también se beneficiarían al aprender nuestro idioma, y su lista de opciones y oportunidades de igual manera se expandiría.

¿Te imaginas qué maravilloso sería ver a más Americanos interesados en nuestra cultura, comprando queso fresco en los súper mercados Latinos, o yendo al cine en español?

www.ingramcontent.com/pod-product-compliance
Lightning Source LLC
LaVergne TN
LVHW051257080426
835509LV00020B/3019